# The Most Important Decision You'll Ever Make

# The Most Important Decision You'll Ever Make

*The Journey to Find and Follow God*

Sanford Zensen

WIPF & STOCK · Eugene, Oregon

THE MOST IMPORTANT DECISION YOU WILL EVER MAKE
The Journey to Find and Follow God

Copyright © 2021 Sanford Zensen. All rights reserved. Except for brief quotations in critical publications or reviews, no part of this book may be reproduced in any manner without prior written permission from the publisher. Write: Permissions, Wipf and Stock Publishers, 199 W. 8th Ave., Suite 3, Eugene, OR 97401.

Wipf & Stock
An Imprint of Wipf and Stock Publishers
199 W. 8th Ave., Suite 3
Eugene, OR 97401

www.wipfandstock.com

PAPERBACK ISBN: 978-1-6667-3300-6
HARDCOVER ISBN: 978-1-6667-2722-7
EBOOK ISBN: 978-1-6667-2723-4

Unless otherwise noted Scripture quotations are taken from the *New American Standard Bible*® (NASB), Copyright © 1960, 1962, 1963, 1968, 1971, 1972, 1973,1975, 1977, 1995 by The Lockman Foundation. Used by permission. www.Lockman.org.

Scripture quotations marked (AMP) are taken from the *Amplified® Bible*, Copyright © 2015 by The Lockman Foundation. Used by permission. www.Lockman.org.

Scripture quotations marked (ESV) are from *The Holy Bible, English Standard Version*® (ESV®), copyright © 2001 by Crossway, a publishing ministry of Good News Publishers. Used by permission. All rights reserved.

Scriptures marked (KJV) are taken from the *King James Version*, public domain.

Scripture quotations marked (MSG) are taken from *The Message*, copyright © 1993, 1994, 1995, 1996, 2000, 2001, 2002 by Eugene H. Peterson. Used by permission of NavPress. All rights reserved. Represented by Tyndale House Publishers, Inc.

Scripture marked (NKJV) taken from the *New King James Version*®. Copyright © 1982 by Thomas Nelson. Used by permission.

Scripture quotations marked (NIV) are taken from the Holy Bible, *New International Version*®, NIV®. Copyright © 1973, 1978, 1984, 2011 by Biblica, Inc.™ Used by permission of Zondervan. All rights reserved worldwide. www.zondervan.com The "NIV" and "New International Version" are trademarks registered in the United States Patent and Trademark Office by Biblica, Inc.™

Scripture quotations marked (NLT) are taken from the Holy Bible, *New Living Translation* Copyright © 1996, 2004, 2007 by Tyndale House Foundation. Used by permission of Tyndale House Publishers Inc., Carol Stream, IL 60188. All rights reserved. New Living, NLT, and the New Living Translation logo are registered trademarks of Tyndale House Publishers.

Scripture quotations marked (Phillips) are taken from *The New Testament in Modern English*, copyright 1958, 1959, 1960 J.B. Phillips and 1947, 1952, 1955, 1957, 1976, The MacMillan Company, New York. Used by permission. All rights reserved.

Scripture quotations marked (TPT) are from *The Passion Translation*®. Copyright © 2017, 2018 by Passion & Fire Ministries, Inc. Used by permission. All rights reserved. ThePassionTranslation.com.

All rights reserved. This book or any portion thereof may not be reproduced or used in any manner whatsoever without the express written permission of the author except for the use of brief quotations in a literary work or book review.

*To my children, Melissa, Eric, and Nathan
that you will make the most important
decision of all — To pursue God and follow
Him faithfully and wholeheartedly all the
days of your life.*

"When you come looking for me, you'll find me. Yes, when you get serious about finding me and want it more than anything else, I'll make sure you won't be disappointed…You can count on it."
—Jeremiah 29:13–14 (MSG)

# A PRAYER
## By Blaise Pascal

Recorded in *The Varieties of Religious Experience* by William James, (New York, NY: Longmans, Green and Company, 1920), 286

*I ask You neither for health nor for sickness, for life nor for death; but that You may dispose of my health and my sickness, my life and my death, for Your glory…You alone know what is expedient for me; You are the sovereign master, do with me according to Your will. Give to me, or take away from me, only conform my will to Yours. I know but one thing, Lord, that it is good to follow You, and bad to offend You. Apart from that, I know not what is good or bad in anything. I know not which is most profitable to me, health or sickness, wealth or poverty, nor anything else in the world. That discernment is beyond the power of men or angels, and is hidden among the secrets of Your providence, which I adore, but do not seek to fathom.*

# TABLE OF CONTENTS

Introduction ..................................................................................... 1
Making the Right Choice — Write Your Own Story ............................ 7
Where in the World Are You Gonna Look? ......................................... 16
God in a Box ..................................................................................... 30
"Are You Guys Ready? Let's Roll!" ..................................................... 44
The Mystery of God .......................................................................... 59
The God Who Put on Skin ................................................................ 75
The Reality of God: The Truth and Nothing But the Truth ............. 87
God Behind the Scenes .................................................................... 98
He Leadeth Me ............................................................................... 108
The Love of My Life ........................................................................ 119
Epilogue .......................................................................................... 127
About the Author ........................................................................... 129
End Notes ....................................................................................... 130

*What Satan put into the heads of our remote ancestors was the idea that they could "be like gods" — could set up on their own as if they had created themselves — be their own masters — invent some sort of happiness for themselves outside God, apart from God. And out of that hopeless attempt has come nearly all that we call human history — money, poverty, ambition, war, prostitution, classes, empires, slavery — the long terrible story of man trying to find something other than God which will make him happy.*[1]

—C.S. Lewis, *Mere Christianity*

# INTRODUCTION

If the truth be told (and I'm a bit embarrassed by this admission), I don't know much about God, at least not as much as I once thought prior to the writing of this book. I have been humbled in the process. John Wesley once stated, "Give me a worm that can understand a man, and I will give you a man who can understand God."[2] That's about how I feel, completely and utterly inadequate when it comes to grasping the depths of the infinite God and His ways. Frankly, I have more questions than I have answers (not unusual for flesh and blood) at this stage of my life. The arrogance of youth has long since faded.

A number of years ago, I asked some college students, "Who is God and what is He like?" One responded, "God is many different things, and I'm still trying to figure it all out." I can relate. Another remarked, "God is an eternal being; someone I will never fully know, comprehend, or wrap my mind around." That describes my thinking on the matter quite accurately. The need to find God and know Him grows with daily experience.

I readily admit my ignorance and lack of understanding of God and the reasons behind His decisions and actions. In short, I need (as we all do) a fuller knowledge of Him, making the search for God an absolute necessity, for in the unveiling of the reality of God, we can

## INTRODUCTION

know something of His love, goodness, power, faithfulness (and so much more), and His desire to want the very best for our daily lives. It is a journey worth taking.

Successful, quality living requires three basic elements: the *knowledge of God* (who God is and how He operates), the *presence of God* (the assurance that God is with us as we walk through life), and the *favor of God* (the guarantee of our success in fulfilling our role and securing our mission in the world). All three are essential for life's adventure.

Moses would not take another step forward in pursuit of Canaan (cf. Exodus 33:13–16), apart from these fundamentals. The journey to the promised land fails without the essentials necessary to change lives for the better, and that is exactly what God wants.

In his book, *The Prodigal God*, Tim Keller reminds us of this:

> *[God's] love can become more real to you than the love of anyone else. It can delight, galvanize, and console you…If you are filled with worry and anxiety, you do not only need to believe that God is in control of history. You must see, with the eyes of the heart, His dazzling majesty. Then you will know He has things in hand."*[3]

Traveling home on a Saturday night, I was listening to Christian radio. The programing was geared specifically toward youth and focused on those teens struggling with some particular, personal issue. It wasn't long before a teenager called the station and shared his heart. Vulnerability is a gutsy move and always frightening, but he wanted and needed help. The disc jockey politely listened, asked a few clarifying questions, and then made an honest effort to counsel and guide the young man through a maze of problems. At the end of the interview, he prayed for the boy, pointing him toward God and the answers he was seeking. His prayer began with the words, "Oh, God, You are so cool." Honestly, I bristled and cringed, thinking at the moment that we need to do better than shallow, popular, trendy cliches and cultural theology when speaking of God and to God. The trap of familiarity and borderline contempt must be resisted. No man should ever take God for granted, for ours is the privilege of gaining entrance into the very throne room of Heaven for an audience with the King. Unfortunately, we have lost a sense of deep reverence and awe and have failed to bow low in humility before the majesty of God.

At Mt. Sinai, Moses cautiously ascended to the top of the mountain to speak with God. The trumpets were blasting. Flashes of lightning cracked across the sky. Fire and smoke engulfed that holy place, and the mountain shook violently. God was present. It must have been unnerving, to say the least. As Moses spoke with God, the Scriptures report that God *"answered him with thunder,"* and the people *"trembled."* The loud rolling sound and slap of thunder would have gotten my attention, too, sending shock waves through my entire being. They were *"terrified."* And why not? They had met God, heard the voice of God, and experienced the holiness and uniqueness of God. They were stunned, their senses overloaded, (cf. Exodus 19:16–20), and their souls were rocked to their very core. The presence and reality of God is breathtaking, even shocking, and definitely disturbing. No one, I might point out, uttered the words, "Oh, God, You're so cool!" Not then. Not ever. A little trembling and humility would be acceptable, maybe preferable, in the presence and pursuit of almighty God, *"the One forming light and creating darkness, causing well-being and creating calamity"* (Isaiah 45:7).

A.W Tozer surmised this:

> *All the problems of Heaven and earth, though they were to confront us together and at once, would be nothing compared with the overwhelming problem of God: That He is, what He is like; and what we as moral beings must do about Him.*[4]

Elijah issued a challenge (more on him later) to a people who were reluctant to recognize the reality and authority of God in their lives. *"How long are you going to sit on the fence? If God is the real God, follow him; if it's Baal, follow him. Make up your minds! And nobody said a word; nobody made a move"* (I Kings 18:21, MSG). And that is precisely the focus and purpose of this book, to move us toward a definitive, decisive decision regarding God, to help us make up our minds about Who He is and what He requires of us, to stop hesitating (*"limping"* is the literal translation) between two opinions and get on with it, and *"search for Him with all your heart and all your soul"* (Deuteronomy 4:29).

There are but two options before us all: 1) Either we settle for business as usual and continue on as we've always been living, missing the miracle and joy of drawing close to God and the benefits thereof, or 2) we decide to take the sacred journey, follow after God as His Spirit leads, learn to lean on His strength, rely on His promises, and trust His faithfulness, wisdom, love, and Word. The time comes to either fish or cut bait. Make your choice. Let's roll! It will be the most important decision you'll ever make — one that will take you on the journey of a lifetime. Seek, find, and follow God.

We have a special invitation from the mouth of Jesus to start the journey. *"Are you tired? Worn out? Burned out on religion? Come to me. Get away with me…Walk with me and work with me—Keep company with me and you'll learn to live freely and lightly"* (Matthew 11:28–30, MSG). God can be found. He is available, approachable, and accessible. Augustine said, "To fall in love with God is the greatest romance; to seek him the greatest adventure; to find him, the greatest human achievement."[5] The most important matter before you is to know God in Christ, the God who *"became flesh…dwelt among us"* so we may *"behold His glory"* (John 1:14) and be well prepared and readied for the long, sometimes hard road ahead. C.H. Spurgeon observed that the heart of a man earnestly seeking God "is hot within him…so mad that [he cries] in the depths of [his] soul."[6] I've done my fair share of crying in my lifetime over what I've done or failed to do. I readily recognize my need for God. I have regrets. *"I know my transgressions, and my sin is ever before me"* (Psalm 51:3). My moral folly lies heavy on my heart. No one has to tell me that I've done wrong and royally screwed up. I know it, and it cuts deep to the "depths of my soul," driving me to the only place where hope reigns and mercy flows — the cross. It is there by the grace of God that I find a release from my past, a full pardon for my morally bankrupt behavior, peace with God and peace with myself, and a fresh new start in life with an eye toward eternity. The key to successful living is found in God, seeking hard after Him, finding Him in your journey, and following Him for the remainder of your days. There is no better way to live.

George Mueller said it this way:

> *The more we know of God, the happier we are. It was when we were in entire ignorance of God that we were without real peace and joy…and the more we become acquainted with Him, the more truly happy we become. What will make us so exceedingly happy in Heaven? It will be the fuller knowledge of God.*[7]

Three-time Super Bowl champion Joe Gibbs met God for the first time as a nine-year-old boy and pledged his life to Christ. It was the start of his journey. But like so many, he stumbled along the way. He admitted, "My college days and the first years of my coaching career didn't reflect [my commitment to God]. Actually, I had been drifting away from the Lord…and (my earlier decision in life) had little impact on my day-to-day living." But God was not finished with the man. There is more.

At a church in Fayetteville, Arkansas, Gibbs came to terms with the emptiness and dissatisfaction of his personal and professional life and confessed that he had not been living for the Lord. In his devotional, *Game Plan for Life*, he wrote of that special moment when God found him once again. "I wish that I had always walked closely with the Lord, but the reality was that I had wasted many years by failing to seek His guidance in every part of my life. This was a turning point for me."[8]

I could have written a similar script. Wasted years. Less-than-stellar behavior. Empty days. I pursued just about everything else except God. It's a good thing He came running after me, like the loving

## INTRODUCTION

father who saw his prodigal son from afar and ran to meet his wayward boy who was heading home.

Go ahead. Start your search. Seek God until you find Him (and you will), and when you do, follow Him. "Let's roll!" Make the most important decision of your life. Meet the challenge. Make up your mind. *"If the Lord is God, follow Him,"* and do what the hymn writer did long ago, "Lord, I would clasp Thy hand in mine."[9] The choice you make now will determine the future course of your life and the destiny of your soul.

> "...*either [you are turning] into a creature that is in harmony with God...or else into one that is in a state of war and hatred with God, and with its fellow-creatures, and with itself. To be the one kind of creature is heaven: that is, it is joy and peace and knowledge and power. To be the other means madness, horror, idiocy, rage, impotence, and eternal loneliness. Each of us at each moment is progressing to one state or the other.*"[1]
>
> —C.S. Lewis, *Mere Christianity*

# 1

# MAKING THE RIGHT CHOICE — WRITE YOUR OWN STORY

The heart cry of the New Testament from Matthew to Revelation is summed up in the command Jesus issued in the Sermon on the Mount, "[All day, every day] *Steep your life in God-reality, God-initiative, God-provisions. Don't worry about missing out. You'll find all your everyday human concerns will be met*" (Matthew 6:33, MSG). The connection between unlocking the best for your life and the choices you and I make daily (particularly in following after God) cannot be overstated.

I recently sat down with an eighty-eight-year-old man with a boatload of life experience behind him. We had a wonderful conversation about faith, following Christ, and living successfully in this world. Let me summarize his thoughts.

> *The most powerful thing in the world is the ability to choose. Every day starts with making a choice about one thing or another — the use of time, money, tasks to be accomplished, travel (where I am going when I head out the door in the morning), the food I eat, picking my friends (who I will hang with today), the level of commitment to my marriage, my church and ministry, my behavior, beliefs, attitudes, and more. Everything hinges on choices, and the ability to choose is present within each of us.*

The capacity to seek God and discover His desire for my life and then choose to either willingly comply with His wishes in every detail and ring the very best out of life, or knowingly opt out of His will and go my own way, remains a sure choice in a moral universe. No pre-programmed, androids here. Every man and woman is presented with both good and bad choices and permitted the opportunities to respond to current circumstances and tomorrow's events as they see fit. The capacity to move one way or the other is what makes daily decisions so very powerful and important. Ultimately, the choices made will determine whether I live successfully in this world and/or the next. My future is before me. I get to write my story and nobody else.

In 2001, thirteen-year-old Stephen Curry was distraught over losing an important AAU basketball game at a tournament in Tennessee. He had played poorly, and the team came up short on the scoreboard. He said it was like "a wake-up call…that I just wasn't good enough." Later that night, while "licking his wounds" and feeling sorry for himself, his mom sat him down and gave him some advice.

> *No one gets to write your story but you. Not some scouts. Not some tournament. Not these other kids, who might do this better or that better…None of those people, and none of those things, gets to be the author of your story. Just you. So think real hard about it. Take your time. And then you go and write what you want to write. But just know that this story — it's yours.*

The seven-time NBA All-Star Curry said, "It's the best advice I've ever gotten. And anytime I've needed it — anytime I've been snubbed, or underrated, or even flat-out disrespected — I've just remembered those words, and I've persevered."[2]

The power to decide where life takes me and where it all ends, rests squarely on my shoulders. Make no mistake. Attitude, actions, happiness, kindness and generosity, giving, obedience, discouragement, jealousy, anger, respect, and love[3] (and more) are the options laid out before us all — every single day, including the decision to involve God or not in my daily routines. That is mine to make, and maybe the most important choice of all. The divine offer remains true for every man and woman. Life or death. The "broad road," which *"leads to disaster"* or the narrow, *"hard road, which leads out into life"* (Matthew 7:13–14, PHILLIPS). Take your pick. Write the story. Follow God.

Near the end of his days, Moses summed up the key to successful daily living in just two words — *"Choose life."* A simple, insightful, uncomplicated life principle.

> **Deuteronomy 30:19–20** – *I have set before you life and death, blessing and curse. Therefore choose life, that you and your offspring may live, loving the Lord your God, obeying His voice, and holding fast to Him, for He is your life and length of days…"*

The point of Christianity is not simply to search for God. The objective is consistent obedience to His laws, which are designed to bring the best of life to those who would follow God's lead. No lip service, please. Compliance with God's Word is what truly matters in the long haul. It gets results. It always has. It always will. His authority and rule over your daily decisions is the most important factor to your well-being. Finding God (or more to the point, when He finds you) is critical, because ultimately, "Father Knows Best" (the title of a TV series aired 1954–1960). That's the secret: recognizing the reality of

God and then changing course, if necessary, and moving in the direction of His leading. Jesus taught that eternal life, in fact all of life, is predicated on knowing and experiencing the Father *"as the only true God, and to know and experience Jesus Christ, as the Son"* (John 17:3, TPT). An intimate knowledge of God and making the right choice to follow Him makes all the difference in the world. It is the right decision, affecting the rest of your life. J. I. Packer gave good advice.

> *Would you lose your sorrow? Would you drown your cares? Then go, plunge yourself in the Godhead's deepest sea; be lost in his immensity; and you shall come forth as from a couch of rest, refreshed and invigorated. I know nothing which can so comfort the soul; so calm the swelling billows of sorrow and grief; so speak peace to the winds of trial, as a devout musing upon the subject of the Godhead.*[4]

A powerful insight.

In the midst of a city whose walls were breached, its buildings set a blaze, and the livelihood of its inhabitants destroyed (cf. Isaiah 24–25), Isaiah proclaimed the biblical principle for living life successfully, even amidst personal hopelessness and terror.

> **Isaiah 26:3–4, MSG** – *People with their minds set on [God], you keep completely whole, [lit. "shalom, shalom"] Steady on their feet, because they keep at it and don't quit. Depend on God and keep at it because in the Lord God you have a sure thing.*

The Scriptures teach that any life centered in God and His lordship over the affairs of daily living is remarkably secure, creating the deepest sense of peace and courage to an anxious mind and a troubled heart. No matter how dismal life may seem, great comfort and encouragement come from knowing that God works *"all things [including the most trying of situations]…for good"* (Romans 8:28), my good. "I have learned," said C. H. Spurgeon, "to kiss the waves that throw me up against the Rock of Ages." The knowledge and presence of God bring real hope in a messed up world, particularly mine, and so I am learning (though not there, yet) to fully depend on Him in every circumstance. I am discovering in my journey that God is worth pursuing because He alone enables me to *"keep at it,"* to keep pressing forward, to keep moving ahead with confidence and a renewed faith through every facet of day-to-day life — from the joys of mountaintop experiences to the unexplained and unexpected trials in the lowest of valleys. God is a *"sure thing."* Go ahead. Take His hand. The best is yet to come.

Heather Bennett found God to be *"a sure thing"* while struggling with despair and the loss of her husband. He died of cancer, leaving her to care for and raise two children. Her story is recorded in *Beyond the Rapids*, a personal record of her journey, her faith, and her discovery that God can be found amidst tragedy. I dare say that moments of heartbreak may provide our best opportunity to experience the presence and strength of God. The following excerpt is from her book:

> *Just as rivers are fed by water that comes from the rains above, I have often wondered if God cries, if His tears parallel our own. Jesus certainly cried after Lazarus died, for it says in John's account of this story that "Jesus wept" (John 11:35), even though he knew that He would raise Lazarus to life. On the day James [Heather's husband] died, as rain fell from the sky, I wondered if God was shedding tears with me, giving me an image of Himself weeping with those who weep, mourning with those who mourn.[5]*

A young woman who desperately searched for God when she needed Him most found Him in the midst of her grief, and there she chose to grasp His hand tightly, and then hang on to a *"sure thing"* — the grace, love, and compassion of God to take her through. It is her story and the right choice. It was her only real choice other than giving way to woeful despair and deep depression. And frankly, she was not about to do that.

Martin Rizzi, campus pastor at The Tabernacle in Buckley, Michigan, wrote the following amidst the upheaval of the Covid-19 pandemic, the spread of the ridiculousness of the cancel culture movement, the loss of Mr. Potato Head, the vilification of Pepe Le Pew, the vandalism and burning of our nation's cities, and a volatile political scene filled with anger, distrust, and questionable, self-serving agendas (just to touch the surface of what we've all experienced to some degree).

> *What if I told you that in the midst of all that has happened in the world, I am not worried? What if I said that nothing of consequence has been shaken? Would you claim I have my head in the sand, or would you assume my foundation is firmly rooted in something unshakable? The truth is that the world is and always has been in turmoil, but I am not surprised or concerned...I am not shaken because I choose [there's that choice factor again] to put my faith in something greater, something that has stood the test of time and is not built on the strength of man, but is inspired by God.*[6]

Faith comes and dramatically increases as you choose to meet and experience God for yourself, resulting in genuine stability and security, and a whole lot less worry. The deeper your relationship with Him, the more you know of His character and faithfulness (something many of us have yet to fully appreciate), the easier it becomes to rely on Him, relax a bit more in a hurried and unpredictable world, and leave matters in God's capable hands. Good choice. Good move. Good foundation for building a quality life, as I write my story rooted in a great God who is trustworthy, good, and *"able to do exceeding abundantly beyond all that we ask or think"* (Ephesians 3:20).

The disciples lost sight of God during a storm (much like the rest of us do) and ran scared, fearing for their lives, though Jesus was present, sleeping comfortably through the relentless pounding of the waves and gale force winds. How typical. Take note here. God is never surprised by trial or chaos (sometimes He creates it), nor does He panic in the face of tribulation and mounting pressures and problems! That's what I do. I fear the worst. I expect the worst, always thinking of a "worst-case scenario." That is one miserable story to write.

That dreadful night aboard a ship that appeared ready to plunge down to a watery grave and end the lives of the disciples struggling to stay afloat, there was no time for intellectual musings or philosophical discussions about the existence of God — not that night, though maybe another night while roasting marshmallows over an open fire with everyone singing "Kumbaya." But on this turbulent, thunderous night, only the frantic search to secure divine assistance in an impossible, worrisome situation made any sense. Either God would move supernaturally to rescue, or He would not. As it stood, all (crew and passengers alike) were going under. Their futures were in jeopardy. Their lives were out of their immediate control. They had no answers. No ability to save themselves. No life preservers. No life guards. No life boats. They needed help and fast, and they knew it, desperately needing to find God amidst all that turmoil. He was their only hope, their last resort. I've been in that storm and on that boat!

Nothing like a little desperation and despair to motivate me to make the right choice and passionately seek divine help from above (cf. Psalm 42:1–3). Typically, panic pushes me (and you) toward God. There is no place to go. When I am at my wit's end, with my life on the line, and seeing no immediate remedy to my problems, I am ready at that point to seek out Christ. He holds the answer to my fears, worries, and doubts. He alone is the revelation of God's power and authority to calm the seas and quiet the storm with but a word. It is what God does, and therefore the right decision, even the smart decision, to seek Him out, follow Him, and leave my life in His strong hands.

St. Richard of Chichester (1197–1253) prayed fervently (the latter part of his prayer sounds much like the lyrics from the old rock musical, Jesus Christ Superstar).

---

*Thanks be to you, my Lord Jesus Christ,*
*For all the benefits you have given me,*
*For all the pains and insults you have borne for me,*
*A most merciful Redeemer, Friend, and Brother,*
*May I know you more clearly,*
*Love you more dearly,*
*Follow you more nearly,*
*Day by day. Amen.*[7]

---

The personal accounts of many individuals stand as a viable and positive witness to the intervening work and character of God through the ages. He has been, He is, and He will forever be intimately present and personally active in all creation, but particularly showing up with an extended hand of divine help for people like you and me trying to make it in this troubled world. God has made Himself accessible and available to men and women from every culture and generation, tribe and nation, from the beginning of time to the end of eternity. C.S. Lewis once advised a friend, "Continue seeking God with seriousness. Unless He wanted you, you would not be wanting (or finding) Him."[8] The reality of the moment, any moment for that matter, is that the hand of God is extended to us all. Nothing has changed since the inception of human history.

Twenty-eight hundred years ago, God sent a message of hope by way of Isaiah to a people held captive in Babylon: *"For I, the Lord your God, hold your right hand; it is I who say to you, 'Fear not, I am the one who helps you'"* (Isaiah 41:13, ESV). God continues to this day to graciously reach out His mighty hand to me and you. Grab hold of it. Don't let go, and let Him take you wherever He wants. You will have no regrets at your journey's end. The greatest fear somebody said is "to go through life living small but not realizing it until it's too late."⁹ No problem with that issue, if you are following God. It's a good story to write.

The challenge issued by Elijah on Mt. Carmel in the ninth century BC is still relevant in today's world, maybe more so than at any other time in human history, and certainly applicable to my own life. *"If the Lord is God, follow him"* (I Kings 18:21, NIV). The story you write, be it good or bad, will depend on the most important decision you will ever make going forward. Follow Him or live as you see fit and go your own way.

---

**Job 23:3, ESV** – *"Oh, that I knew where I might find Him."*

---

*"Everything else in life can wait, but the search for God cannot wait."*[1]

—George Harrison, shortly before he died

# 2

# WHERE IN THE WORLD ARE YOU GONNA LOOK?

The movie, *Wide Awake* (written and directed by M. Night Shyamalan), is about a Catholic school boy named Joshua, who is pictured frantically searching for God. He started his journey to find God because he specifically wanted to know whether or not his deceased grandfather was okay. Joshua and his ten-year-old friend Dave are sitting in a garage having a discussion.

"You know what, Dave? I'm going on a mission. A real mission."

"What kind of mission?" Dave wants to know.

"The kind where you're looking for something important."

"What are you gonna look for?"

"God."

"God? What for?"

"I just want to talk to him."

"Why?"

"To make sure my grandpa is okay."

Dave replies, "Remember when you told me I was stupid for staring at that bug lamp on my porch for six hours hoping the purple light would have gamma rays and turn me into the Incredible Hulk so I could fight crime? Your mission is more stupid than that."

"Why?" Joshua asks.

"'Cause you can't look for God."

"Why not?"

"Where in the world are you gonna look?"[2]

Let me answer the question (which is a really good one, by the way). The search begins and ends in the pages of Scripture where the historical, indestructible, accurate record of Jesus, the prophets, and the saints of old are preserved in written form for all to see. Norman Geisler and William Nix wrote this in *A General Introduction to the Bible*:

> *There are no good reasons to suppose that the authors of Scripture were not honest and sincere men…What shall be made of men — who claim as evidence for the divine authority of their message that they saw Jesus of Nazareth, crucified under Pontius Pilate, alive and well? What shall be made of that claim that they saw Him on about a dozen occasions over a period of a month and a half? That they talked with Him, ate with Him, saw His wounds, and handled Him, and even the most skeptical among them fell at His feet and cried, "My Lord and my God!"*[3]

Frankly, there is no other reliable place to look for the answers to the great issues of life, death, and eternity and the identity and character of God Himself. It's all found in the Scriptures and ultimately in the person of Christ, as well as in the lives of countless people throughout history who have experienced God for themselves.

The renowned theologian Cornelius Van Til wrote, "I have never met Christ in the flesh. No matter, He has written me a letter. Not he, Himself. He chose helpers. By His Spirit, the Spirit of truth, these helpers wrote what He wanted me to know."[4]

The God of creation and redemption can be found in the events of the Garden of Eden reported by Moses in the opening pages of Genesis, implicating Adam and Eve who initially got themselves (and the rest of us) in big trouble. But the story does not stop there. God steps out of the shadows to reveal His mercy and lays out the basics of His redemptive plan — the *"seed of the woman"* (Jesus) would one day crush the head of the serpent (Genesis 3:15), destroy the works of the devil, bring the kingdom of God to earth, and salvage mankind. From the very beginning, the power of the cross and the glory of the resurrection went on display, pointing to a place called Calvary and an empty, borrowed tomb. No god other than *Elohim* has ever loved so deeply or cared so much for His creation and creatures, even in the face of "cosmic treason," which ruled the day from then until now, leaving death and destruction behind everywhere to mar the lives of men and women across all cultural, socio-economical, and generational boundaries. *"There is no one who always does what is right, no, not even one"* (Romans 3:10) — an "indictment," wrote Carl Barth, that "the whole course of human history pronounces…against itself."[5] Essentially, we are guilty of "thumbing our nose" in the face of God. Still, God wants to draw near. He wants to be found. We just need to know where to look.

For most of us non-scholar types, I might suggest that the hunt begin in a Bethlehem manger where a King was born who would change the world for the better and rescue a wayward people from the consequences of their foolhardy behavior. The biblical record takes us to a wedding in Cana where water is miraculously turned into the best wine of the day. The search resumes at the water's edge of the Jordan River where Jesus was seen being baptized by John, and then continues to the synagogues to hear Christ speak with authority like no one else before Him. Journey to the Northwest shore of the Sea of Galilee where five thousand, hungry people were fed with a few loaves of bread and two fish (cf. Matthew 14:13–21). Observe Jesus healing a paralyzed man. Listen to His words, *"My Son, your sins are forgiven"* (Mark 2:5). Some in the crowd admitted, *"We have never seen anything like this"*

(Mark 2:12), and indeed, they had not. Only God could do and say such things.

Head out from the streets of Capernaum and journey to the tomb of Lazarus located in the village of Bethany, where Mary and Martha and their neighbors were weeping over the loss of a brother and friend. There in the darkest of hours, surrounded my hopelessness and despair, you can find God standing outside the grave of a man who had died four days earlier, calling forth new life. *"Lazarus, come out…Unwrap him, and let him go"* (John11:43–44, NLT)! *"Let him go"* is the heartbeat and mission of Christ. Many who witnessed the event that day *"believed in Him"* (John 11:45) — the *"Resurrection and the life"* (cf. John 11:25–44). If you know Jesus and have heard Him speak, and have watched Him move with power and purpose through the streets of the ancient and modern world and in the lives of people broken in body and spirit, be assured you have found God. You have discovered the God Who is still in the business of raising the dead and impacting the lives of men and women for the better.

Eventually, the search for God will bring you to Golgotha to that holy hill where Jesus willingly stretched out His hands in love divine. *"Father forgive them; they do not know what they're doing"* (Luke 23:34–35, TPT). Stay at the cross for a moment and listen to the testimony of the centurion who stood in the shadow of the crucified Christ, the sacrificial Lamb of God, and declared with no bias and personal agenda, *"Truly, this man was the Son God"* (Mark 15:39). Catch the words of the thief, a convicted felon, executed next to Jesus. The criminal begged Him for mercy (something we all need) and got it. Then hurry without delay to the place where Jesus was buried, and there find a large, heavy stone stamped with a Roman seal to warn people to keep out (Matthew 27:62–66). It once covered the entrance of the guarded tomb, but now the stone had been rolled away and inside an angel, appearing as a *"young man sitting at the right"* (Mark 16:5) as you enter the burial chamber, ready to make the greatest announcement of hope ever heard by those *"looking for Jesus the Nazarene"* (Mark 16:6). The good news was clearly proclaimed that sacred morning, *"He has risen; He is not here"* (Mark 16:6. NASB).

Five hundred people (cf. I Corinthians 15:1–8), including the women who first arrived at the tomb, and *"all the apostles,"* and Peter, Thomas, Nathaniel, and *"two others"* who will attest to the fact that they had breakfast with Jesus along the banks of the Sea of Tiberias (cf. John 21:1–14) — each one a personal witness to having seen and met the risen Lord. The grave remains empty. Take a look inside, as countless others before you. Search where you must. You will not find Him, for death could not hold Him. The tomb is unoccupied. He is alive forever more.

Chuck Colson wrote in his book, *The Faith: What Christians Believe, Why They Believe It, And Why It Matters*:

> *I know the resurrection is a fact, and Watergate proved it to me. How? Because twelve men testified they had seen Jesus raised from the dead, then they proclaimed that truth for forty years, never once denying it. Everyone was beaten, tortured, stoned and put in prison. They would not have endured that if it weren't true. Watergate embroiled twelve of the most powerful men in the world — and they couldn't keep a lie for three weeks. You're telling me twelve apostles could keep a lie for forty years? Absolutely impossible."*[6]

Comb through the historical records and the teachings of Christ substantiated and verified by eyewitness accounts and preserved in Holy Writ. Consider the dramatic change in the temperament and the lives of the apostles following the crucifixion and resurrection of Christ — men who were once hopeless and distraught over the death of the Master, now suddenly alive, more alive than ever before, empowered, excited, confident in the person of Jesus and the message of the gospel, willing to risk all for the truth surrounding the grace and love of God. J.D. Greer said, "The resurrection means the gospel is power—not just another competing theory of religion, but a new way to live."[7]

The pages of Scripture are where you must go to look for God and read His story. The Bible was written over the course of some 1400 to 1600 years, by forty different authors — shepherds, fishermen, kings, an Internal Revenue agent, and a fig picker (just to name a few); all from varying socio-economic backgrounds and three different continents — Asia, Africa, and Europe; all declaring the same theme, about the same God; all focusing on the same divine purpose — to *"proclaim joyous news* [to all creation]…*Here is your God"* (Isaiah 40:9), the One Who promises *to "hold you by the hand and watch over you"* (Isaiah 42:6), rescue you, forgive you, bury your sin in the deepest ocean, remove your shame and guilt, restore your self-respect, and set you once again on your feet to walk in newness of life, as God intended. The promises of God are relevant and applicable to modern living, encouraging, comforting, convicting, and challenging to the would-be seeker and follower of Christ.

Hear the testimony of eyewitness accounts, from the early days of the prophets and the Apostles who walked with Jesus to the current era of saints, all of whom can testify to God being true and faithful over the years. The stories are nothing short of phenomenal.

On October 10, 1821, the twenty-nine-year-old lawyer Charles Grandison Finney headed out into the woods near his home in search of God. His intention was to return to his home only if he could fully give his heart to God and follow His lead. Finney was a man determined, motivated, and wholly dedicated to the task at hand. After some hours, he made his way back, convinced of Christ and committed to God's Word and God's work. Later he would write, "The Holy Spirit…seemed to go through me, body and soul. I could feel the impression, like a wave of electricity, going through and through me. Indeed it seemed to come in waves of liquid love, for I could not express it in any other way." He left the courtroom to become the Father of American Revivalism, paving the way for D. L. Moody, Billy Sunday, and Billy Graham,[8] a testimony to the reality of God, the transforming power of the gospel, and the ministry of the Holy Spirit — repeated many times over throughout the history of humankind.

Fred Mendrin did time in San Quentin and Folsom Prison, initially serving a sentence of ten years and seven months for drug possession and later for first-degree murder of a fellow inmate. Prison life was horrible — gangs, stabbings, deadly rivalries, fighting, the constant fear, overwhelming despair, and endless hopelessness. Gang members wanted him dead, but God protected him. God mercifully jumped into the thick of it and found Fred one night sitting alone in his cell, a man shackled by his past, despondent about his life, robbed of a future, uncertain about tomorrow, and desperately wanting a change. This is how he described his conversion:

*I didn't see lights or hear music, but suddenly, the Holy Spirit regenerated my dead spirit and made me alive. I realized, Wow, I believe in God. I believe in Jesus Christ as my Savior. A peace of mind that I never experienced before came over me, and I knew what I needed to do.*

He told one inmate, "I'm a Christian now. That's the life I'm gonna live." Following his release, Fred worked for Prison Fellowship.

*Whenever I have the opportunity to share my story...I take advantage of it. I tell them, "If I can do it, you can do it. I'm no spiritual giant. I am just a sinner saved by the grace of God...Without God, where would I be? Knowing where I've been and where I am now, all I can say is, 'Praise God.'"*[9]

This is not Fred's story. It is God's story of redemption, repeated again and again countless times in the lives of fallen men and women from every generation. It is the story told by the biblical writers inspired by God to write down everything God wanted and wants to say. You can't miss it.

Take a close look at the pronouncements and fulfillment of a multitude of prophecies given hundreds of years before the events took place. Take note of the confirmation of the Patriarchs (Abraham, Isaac, and Jacob) who attest to the reality of God and His intervention in their personal lives. *"Everything you read [in the Scriptures] points to me,"* said Jesus, *"yet you still refuse to come to me so I can give you the life you're looking for—eternal life"* (John 5:39, TPT).

Examine the discoveries of modern-day archeology, all confirming the biblical record as a detailed, accurate, genuine, authentic, credible, reliable source written for the ordinary man on the street, telling the story of the God of redemption. Peter S. Williams, Assistant Professor in Worldviews and Communication at Gimlekollen NLA College, Norway, opened his book, *Digging for Evidence*, with a quote by Millar Burrows, Professor of Archaeology, Yale University, who said:

> *On the whole... archaeological work has unquestionably strengthened confidence in the reliability of the scriptural record...Archaeology has in many cases refuted the views of modern critics.*[10]

Further, there are 5,366 partial and complete New Testament manuscripts and scrolls "copied by hand from the second through the fifteenth centuries."[11] That's impressive. Of all the ancient documents currently available, the Scriptures remain both remarkably steady and historically sure. "Faith," wrote Randall Price in his *Handbook of Biblical Archeology*, "has a factual component."[12] If you look for Jesus between the front and back covers of the Bible, which was written in the past, you will find God in the present. Heaven and earth will pass away, but not the Word of the living God.

Stephen, one of seven deacons appointed to serve the needs of widows in the first-century church, was *"[a man] of good reputation...and of wisdom...full of faith and of the Holy Spirit"* (Acts 6:3, 5) — a remarkable resume by any standard. A man of character with a solid reputation.

He *"performed many astonishing signs and wonders and mighty miracles among the people"* (v. 8, TPT). Regardless of his positive impact in the community, Stephen was hauled off to stand trial before the Sanhedrin to give an account of his faith in Christ and his actions. He came under enormous pressure to disavow his faith. Men from the local synagogue *"rose up and argued with [him]"* (Acts 6:9), threatening his life. But Stephen knew the reality of God, that "God is" — a faithful God, intimately acquainted and involved in the affairs of his life. He had seen *"the glory of God, and Jesus standing at the right hand of God"* (Acts 7:55), which served to confirm and secure the most important decision he had ever made or would make — the decision to follow Christ. The revelation of God in Christ will transform and strengthen the man who has discovered God and will enable that man/woman to find the guts and courage to do what God has called him/her to do — die to self and live for God.

A hateful, angry crowd, *"grinding their teeth at him"* (Acts 7:54), was screaming for blood, demanding his death. Eventually, they dragged him outside the city gates to be stoned. But Stephen dug in — unafraid and more determined than ever to be God's man, divinely assigned and dedicated to deliver God's message, come what may.

His task and future were certain. His eyes were set toward the cross. Jesus *said "If you truly want to follow me, you should at once completely reject and disown your own life. And you must be willing to share my cross and experience it as your own, as you continually surrender to my ways"* (Matthew 16:24, PTP). Stephen would not run from the truth or his appointed end. To the contrary, he stood his ground, fully committed to the Christ of the gospels and the story of redemption. He had found God, understood the cost of discipleship, and opted to follow God's lead, doing what most of us were/are not willing to do or could do in our own strength — forgiving those hell-bent on killing him for his commitment and loyalty to God. I feel dwarfed in the presence of such great faith and strength of character, loving God earnestly and loving people unconditionally.

As he breathed his last, his face bloodied and his body bruised and broken, Stephen glanced heavenward (a good place for the rest of us to look in days of trouble) and saw the splendor of the God he served, the God Who rose from His throne and stood on His feet to honor and applaud the man who would dare to live and die for the sake of Christ, ready to depart this world and all that he once held so dear to follow God to the grave and the gates of the celestial city. Nowhere else do we find the incarnate God, Jesus of Nazareth, standing for any man for whatever reason. He is normally seated *"at the right hand of the Majesty on high"* (cf. Hebrews 1:3; Colossians 3:1), a clear, definitive sign of supremacy, unmatched authority, and unimaginable power, an incredible vision of the One who rules from everlasting to everlasting, the One Who must *"have first place in everything"* (Colossians 1:18), and that includes my life (and yours, too).

In those final minutes, paused on the threshold of eternity, Stephen came face to face with the immensity and dominion of God over the entire universe, and especially his own life. Everything paled in comparison. He saw God and recognized His work — ordaining, orchestrating, and calculating every event taking place, declaring the end from the beginning, and bringing all things (good or bad) in line with His perfect will and ultimate plan. Nothing was haphazard. Nothing was left to chance. God does not work that way. The outcome was already divinely determined. Stephen would follow God anywhere (as we all must), ready to do whatever God would ask of him, even giving his very life for the advancement of God's kingdom and the cause of Christ. *"Whoever loses his life for my sake will find it"* (Matthew 10:30, EVS). Seeking, finding, and following God demands absolute surrender to Him and His plan. Do that, and you will most certainly find God in the good times and in the most difficult and trying of circumstances.

Hanna Whitall Smith, the American evangelist and reformer in the Holiness movement of the nineteenth century, said, "Nothing else is needed to quiet all your fears, but just this, that GOD IS."[13] Maybe that's where I need to be looking more closely — at the details of my daily life — where I've been (embarrassed about that), where I am (thinking I could do better), and where I am headed (a bit more hopeful). I find it necessary to frequently remind myself that God does in fact exist, that "He is," that *"He is [after all] a rewarder of those who seek Him"* (cf. Hebrews 11:6), and then make a firm decision to follow Him to the end.

D.L. Moody said, "We ought to see the face of God every morning before we see the face of man."[14] With the rising of the sun each day, the pursuit of God and the desire to follow Him must begin anew. It must be life's greatest priority the moment my feet hit the floor to start the most important journey any man can take — the search for the person of God, the revelation of His heart, and ultimately, the plan He has for my daily life. It is the road down which Stephen traveled, the same road I must also walk — in utter relinquishment of my will to the good and perfect will of God. I want in on whatever God is up to — loving unconditionally, forgiving fully, healing the brokenhearted, restoring health to the sick, releasing men and women from the prison of their own fears and failures, setting people free to negotiate life anew through the power and message of the gospel and equipping each one to successfully handle whatever might come their way. That's the God I want to serve and follow *"always, even to the end of the age"* (Matthew 28:20). But it's going to take more than lip service to get the job done.

Five young men had the guts to fly into the Ecuadorian Amazon unarmed, for the sole purpose of delivering the message of the love of God to the war-like Auca Indians, a people who lived in constant fear and tribal conflict. The men entered the jungle armed only with their knowledge of God and the power of His transforming mercy and grace. They had their mission. They knew what God wanted done and readied themselves to journey under the banner of the cross and the love of God. Fully aware of the risks to follow God's leading into uncharted waters, they went anyway. Remarkable. Courageous. Selfless. It's what happens when you first meet God, *"(the) King (whose) tender love for us continues on forever!"* (Psalm 136:1–3, TPT).

Long before these men ever touched down in the Amazon, I suspect that each one had a life-changing, one-on-one encounter with

God, and then made their decision to follow wherever God would lead — to the homeless, the prisons, Wall Street, or to the poor living on the streets of Calcutta…wherever, as God wills, even to the rain forests of the Amazon. Theirs was a deliberate and calculated choice to care for the well-being of a jungle tribe, no matter the cost. That was their holy task — to give their lives sacrificially and unselfishly that others might live abundantly, a sobering moment for any individual who decides to surrender to the call of God. It was and is the most important decision a man or woman will ever make.

The journey may take you to the mountaintops of exhilaration and gratification or to the lowest valley where death, suffering, and pain is commonplace. In either case, the total abandonment of self is required and necessary to find God and be used of Him to bring a little bit of heaven to earth. The men made their choice, entered the jungle, and were mercilessly attacked and speared to death by the tribesmen — a seemingly needless and senseless tragedy.

However, the story did not end there. God had other plans. He always does. The sacrifice made that fateful day opened a road paved by the blood of those who would dare to respond to the divine call to bring the redemptive love of God to a people damned for their reckless behavior and heartless deeds (much like the rest of us). What happens next defies human comprehension.

Remarkably, the wife of one and sister of another of these five men returned to the jungle to carry out the mission started by these five selfless missionaries. The women had but one purpose — to love and forgive the very people who had murdered their loved ones and left their children fatherless, and share the gospel of Christ. They knew what God desired above all — that no one should *"perish, but everyone* [including the Aucas] *to come to repentance"* (I Peter 3:9, NIV) and live a full, satisfying life in this world and the next. An entire village was miraculously transformed by the love of God and the gospel of Christ and the efforts of those who knew God and were willing to follow Him back to the jungles, risking all once again to advance His kingdom and change the lives of so many.[15] No one does such things for a lie or a fabricated story.

Jim Elliot, as well as the other four souls who lost their lives that day, were simple, humble men, wanting little more than to serve the God they had found and known some years earlier. Before that final mission, Elliot was heard to say, "Forgive me for being so ordinary while claiming to know so extraordinary a God."[16] Frankly, there was nothing ordinary about any of them. When common men and women find and encounter the uncommon God of the Bible, they live extraordinary lives that produce exceptional results. So will you.

Most of us don't fly off to the jungles to discover and serve God. We live ordinary, routine lives — until that special, miracle moment when God taps us on the shoulder, and we turn to meet and know God in Christ. *"Whenever a person turns to the Lord, the veil is taken away"* and a blind "heart" sees (cf. II Corinthians 3:15–16, NASB 1995). "I once was blind, but now I see" are the words of an old slave trader who encountered Christ. *Amazing Grace!* The moment you choose God, life changes. Priorities, worldview, attitudes and actions will be altered dramatically forever. You can no longer remain the same. The *"old things"* pass away (cf. II Corinthians 5:15), and frankly, it's a good thing.

Choose Christ. Today and tomorrow will be better than you ever thought possible. Not perfect, but better and improving with each passing year. You will love more deeply and faithfully, serve others with energy and enthusiasm, treat people with dignity and respect, and discover your place in the world. Mercy will find you. Compassion will be your guide. Hope will rise up within you. Joy will increase. *"Surely goodness and lovingkindness will follow [you] all the days of [your] life"* (Psalm 23:6), as you follow God even to the jungles of Ecuador. Even there you can find God.

That's the divine promise — *"our lives gradually becoming brighter and more beautiful as God enters our lives and we become like him"* (II Corinthians 3:18, MSG), and all of it coming from the empowering and prompting of God Himself, pressing you and me to search hard until we find Him and are energized toward a decision to follow and serve. *"If the Lord is God, follow Him!"* The words of Elijah continue to ring true.

Os Guinness spoke of our search in terms of "answering the call of our Creator…the ultimate 'why' for living, the highest source of purpose in human existence."[17] Anything less than God will leave us wanting and disappointed because nothing in this world truly and deeply satisfies. *"For all that the world can offer us — the gratification of our flesh, the allurement of the things of the world, and the obsession with status and importance…are in the process of passing away, but those who love to do the will of God live forever"* (I John 2:16–17, TPT).

Our real joy, suggests J.R.R. Tolkien, lies "beyond the walls of the world"[18] with God and God alone, making the search for Him the only thing that makes sense in light of a transitory, empty, and secular worldview that promises much but delivers so little. First, last, and always, make the pursuit of God a major priority in your daily life. The knowledge of Him and His character, and the depth of your encounter with God, will determine the course and quality of your life the rest of your days. You just need to know where to look and then make the most important decision of your life — pursue God.

*"You can't handle the truth!"*[1]
— Jack Nicholson in *A Few Good Men*

# 3

## GOD IN A BOX

Let's face it. No one has God figured out. I certainly don't. Maybe that's why Jesus invited us all to seriously consider *"learning"* about God from Him — an invitation (actually, an imperative) for every anxious, wandering soul looking for *"rest"* (cf. Matthew 11:29–30, ESV) in this crazy, mixed up world. Apparently, knowing God intimately and the ability to rest from the worries and heartaches of the day are intricately tied together, which only serves to heighten the need to find and connect with Him, especially as important and sometimes crucial life decisions are being made daily. I need to know what God thinks on any particular matter. It is critical to any person's success and well-being.

In his classic, *Names of God in the Old Testament*, Nathan J. Stone wrote "The knowledge of God is more essential for the Christian, and indeed for all the world, than the knowledge of anything else — yes, of all things together."[2] Yet, no one has ever gotten a firm grip on the extent of God's being, or gained an unobstructed view of His person, or has been able to fully extract from the heart of God the purity of His motives and the specifics of His plans. We wouldn't know what we were looking at or Who we are looking for anyway. We need some help digging into the *"depths of God"* as we scour the universe searching for the *"limits of the Almighty."* They are *"high as the heavens…deeper than Sheol* [the abode of the dead], *longer than the earth…and broader than the sea"* (Job 11:7–9). I am reminded of an old Sunday school chorus I used to sing as a child: "Deep and wide, deep and wide, there's a fountain flowing deep and wide."

Our understanding of Who God is and how He works is not much better or clearer than "deep and wide." Left to my own devices, the prospects of taking hold of *"the fullness of God,"* residing only in Christ (cf. Colossians 1:19, NLT), is not terribly good. My attempts to better clarify and understand the why, how, and what specifically that God is doing in the world and in my life are like trying to catch a fly with chop sticks (remember Miyagi of the *Karate Kid* movies). The god of my limited thinking is just that, "limited" — much too small and certainly anything but the "Real Thing" (the 1969 marketing slogan for Coca-Cola). John Piper suggested that "the key to Christian living is a hunger and thirst for God," but the problem, he suggests, is that our "hunger and thirst is so small."[3] I think the issue goes deeper. The trouble is that we habitually look for God as we want Him to be, doing what we want Him to do. We lack interest in seeking God as He is, and like most, I tend to put God in a box. It never works very well. He usually breaks out.

A former student of mine observed his two-year-old son licking the flavor off each Pringles chip and then putting them back in the can. The boy's father wondered whether we do the same thing in our relationship with God and our knowledge of Him — taste the good stuff God brings to our lives and then shove him back into a box. We miss experiencing Him as He is. Guilty as charged.

I can *"taste and see that the Lord is good"* (Psalm 34:8, NIV), but not much more than that. Predicting His decisions on a day-to-day basis? Forget it. Understand the reasoning behind His specific purpose and detailed plans for my life and for those that I love? Not happening. He is full of surprises and acts in ways far above my human capabilities and understanding. We just don't know what to do with God.

He defies intellectual definitions and emotional explanations, no matter how passionate and reasonable they may appear to the human psyche. All attempts to take hold of divinity are seriously deficient and lacking in substance. Our minds cannot think that big. Our imaginations are short on ideas. When it comes to God, we lack clarity and precision, which are products of our own sinfulness and flesh and blood. Moreover, finite creatures cannot connect with the concept of infinity and just how big (immense) and unique (holy) God truly is. *"No one,"* wrote John, *"has ever [fully/completely* — perfect tense here] *seen God"* (I John 4:12, cf. also John 1:18), and yet we insist again and again on making God out to be no better than, no more majestic than, no more credible than a "golden calf," created in the fires of our own imaginations. The best we can come up with is a host of "Counterfeit Gods" (a book by Tim Keller worth reading).

C.S Lewis, "the most dejected and reluctant convert in all England," (his words, not mine) said he was surprised by God's humility to accept a "convert" like himself — one who "had always wanted, above all things, not to be 'interfered with…(and) wanted (a mad wish) to call my soul my own." Like most of us, a "prodigal…kicking, struggling, resentful, and darting his eyes in every direction for a chance of escape,"[4] Lewis was caught off guard and could not wrap his mind around a God of such lovingkindness and mercy. I still don't get it, and neither did he — why in the world would God want any of us, especially me, a *"sheep…gone astray"* (Isaiah 53:6) and redeem my miserable life, sacrificially giving His only Son as a ransom to free my imprisoned soul from the power and penalty of my sin — the innocent for the guilty? It's beyond me that God would offer me a pardon, knowing my checkered past, moral shortcomings, poor choices, rebellious and destructive behavior patterns, and sees my failure not as a reason to condemn me, but as a predictor of what He can do and wants to do with my future. I see my guilt (always have) and deeply feel my shame, but God looks beyond that mess and sees Christ, *"crushed"* for my sins (every last one of them), *"pierced through for our* [my] *transgressions"* (Isaiah 53:5), that I might be made *"completely whole"* (Isaiah 53:4–5, TPT), without blemish or stain, and able to *"stand in the presence of His glory blameless with great joy"* (Jude 24). Apparently, God sees what my sin would not ever permit me to see — the truth…that God holds every one of us in great value and counts us worthy to be called the sons and daughters of the Most High. The cross makes that abundantly clear. We are, after all is said and done, highly esteemed and important to Him.

There are no adequate explanations for God's amazing grace other than this plain, unencumbered statement — *God shows His love and mercy because He wants to.* That's it. No reasons given. No clarification is offered or necessary. It is simply His good pleasure to do so. Nothing else. End of story.

*"But God demonstrates His own love toward us, in that while we were yet sinners* [transgressors of divine law, helpless and hopeless, and rebellious toward God], *Christ died for us"* (Romans 5:8). And here is good news: *There is therefore now no condemnation for those who are in Christ Jesus"* (Romans 8:1). Incredible. Mysterious. The love of God *"covers a multitude of sins"* (I Peter 4:8, NIV). A God you cannot imagine and a love you cannot possibly fathom. God does not fit in boxes made by man.

Os Guinness and John Seel warned:

> *Christendom is becoming a betrayal of the Christian faith of the New Testament…In the biblical view, anything created [i.e. relationships, wealth, position, status, etc.] — anything at all that is less than God…can become idolatrous if it is relied upon inordinately until it becomes a full-blown substitute for God and, thus, an idol. The first duty of believers is to say yes to God; the second is to say no to idols.*[5]

Hanna Rosin, staff writer for the Washington Post, wrote twenty years ago of a husband and wife who rejected the church and traditional beliefs and spent years searching for God. In the process, the pair tossed out the parts of Christianity they didn't particularly like (a common practice for many). It's like reading the Bible with a bottle of Whiteout at your side, blotting out passages, whole sections, and entire chapters — anything you find unacceptable and troubling. I suspect that most of the Sermon on the Mount was probably missing from their "version" of the Scriptures, particularly the parts about loving your enemies or blessing those who curse you (cf. Matthew 5:44, Luke 6:28). I'm not particularly fond of these either, but they are part of God's revealed Word, which He expects us to obey. A.W. Tozer foretold our current social climate, when he said, "Not wanting to appear judgmental, we (believers) mistakenly try to make biblical truth fit the culture around us."[6] A serious indictment and a common practice among some churchgoers.

In any case, the couple had no use for the reality of Hell and the judgement of God. I might add as a side note here that I've never conducted or attended a funeral where anyone present ever thought the deceased was any place other than Heaven — no matter how morally bankrupt they may have lived. Nonetheless, the Scriptures teach that *"everyone has to die once, then face the consequences* [the judgement of God]*"* (Hebrews 9:27, MSG). A sobering reality.

Like so many others in today's world, who live life independent of the authority of God and His Word, the two in question rejected the justice and righteousness of God that holds people to the standard of His moral laws and accountable for their personal actions and decisions. They did, however, retain what they liked. "They kept Jesus because Jesus is big on love." Nothing new here. In the current culture, spirituality has become a trip to a religious smorgasbord, picking and choosing our favorites and abandoning the rest. Rosen summarized the results of the couple's search — a perfect example of putting God in a box.

*Now they commune with a new God, a gentle twin of the one they grew up with. He is wise but soft-spoken, cheers them up when they're sad, laughs at their quirks. He is, most essentially, validating, like the greatest of friends. And best of all, He had*

> *been there all along. "We discovered the God within," said Joanne. "That's why we need God. Because we are God. God gives me the ability to create my own godliness."*[7]

Hardly the God of Abraham, Isaac, and Jacob, Who sent the Angel of Death to the households of Egypt, nor the God of the New Testament portrayed as a *"consuming fire"* (Hebrews 12:29). This is not some cosmic teddy bear to cuddle. Yes, God is love, and we see that at the cross of Christ; but this is also a holy God of judgement, and as such, we are warned, *"It is a fearful thing to fall into the hands of the living God"* (Hebrews 10:31). "God is the only comfort," said Lewis, "He is also the supreme terror: the thing we most need and the thing we most want to hide from. He is our only possible ally, and we have made Him our enemy."[8]

A young man earnestly searching for the truth about Who God is and what He is like asked me, "What was the personality of Jesus like?" I responded this way:

> *So often, Jesus is presented as one who sweeps "sin" under the rug; who is morally weak; who lets anything, and everything go (genuine love does not do that); who is non-confrontational, compliant, soft, and non-hostile — like an old, benevolent man shuffling through life unaware of the world around him. Yes, God is love, and He loves each of us right where we are, but that is only part of the story. Balance is required.*

> *Make no mistake. The Jesus in the Gospels, the one who challenges evil and confronts wrongdoing and wrong thinking — the kind that destroys lives — does so motivated by His redeeming, matchless love and divine justice. He gets righteously angry with sin and those who would promote prejudices of all kinds, hatred, selfishness, greed, injustice, and all the rest; and He does so because He sees and understands evil's destructive nature and the consequences it brings to all humanity. The God*

> *who sees all this and fails to act, who fails to get angry at the horror before Him is unworthy to be called "God" for He has not acted like the King of the universe enthroned on high!*

There has never been a shortage of fabricated gods. I can make a box (with the best of them) to put God in, utilizing all the "materials" that make sense to me personally or make me feel good and happy in the moment. Standards of right and wrong (what God requires of us) have become individualized. Authentic discipleship has been replaced by conformity to whatever our subculture deems okay.⁹ Christian theology (what the Scriptures say about God) is marginalized and discarded as irrelevant and outdated. The richness and fullness of God has escaped our eyes, and we are in danger of losing any sense of the transcendence and uniqueness of our Creator. *"I am the Lord; that is my name! I will not give my glory to anyone else, nor share my praise with carved idols* [nor any other god created in the mind and imagination of man]*"* (Isaiah 42:8, NLT).

In fact, whatever we conceive God to be, and make no mistake about this, He is more, much more. He continues incomprehensible, defies definition, and remains a mystery. *"His greatness is unsearchable,"* wrote the psalmist (Psalm 145:3), yet knowing God is Someone we must pursue. The good news is that *"He is not far from each one of us"* (Acts 17:28), which suggests that He is recognizable and welcoming.

At times, we have caught glimpses of God when we have witnessed and experienced first-hand the love of God manifested in and through the lives of God's people (cf. I John 4:16), whose selfless acts of compassion and mercy reveal the nature and character of their Creator. God is also detected in those unusual, unexpected events that occur at special moments, when the miraculous breaks through the *Dark Night of the Soul* (a sixteenth century poem by John of the Cross) and makes a difference in people's troubled lives.

Israel was up to its knees in Egyptian mud trying to make straw into bricks, when God supernaturally stepped into their sorrow and difficulties and liberated an entire nation after four hundred years of slavery. Subsequently, they marched out as victors from under the taskmaster's whip and headed for the promised land. It was a demonstration of the power and faithfulness of God to those who would seek Him and find Him along life's journey.

There is still more to see and know of God — the healing of a man born blind, the raising of a Jairus' daughter, the calming of a storm at sea, the healing of Peter's mother-in-law who was sick with fever, a neighbor unexpectedly showing up with boxes of groceries for hungry orphans because men like George Mueller prayed for God's help, or a friend arriving unannounced at the home of a widow to dry her tears and help fill the emptiness of a lonely heart — all of which gives us a sense of Who God is, how He works, and what He is about. And some of us still don't get it. God cannot be boxed in. He does what pleases Him and for reasons oftentimes known only to Him.

At the Institution for Mechanical Engineers in London, John Lennox, a Christian author and professor of mathematics at the University of Oxford, and Michael Ruse, professor of philosophy of science at Florida State University, participated in a debate titled *"Science, Faith, and the Evidence for God."* Ruse argued that the miracles of Jesus didn't physically occur. They weren't literal, as recorded in the New Testament, but rather literary descriptions/examples of the positive influence Christ's teachings had on the people with whom He came in contact on a daily basis. Ruse explained the feeding of the 5,000 by dismissing the supernatural element of the event with the wave of his anti-supernatural hand. He said, "[Jesus] filled people with love, so that the people who had brought food shared it with those who didn't have it…that for me is a real miracle"[10] Nice thought, but the downside of human history and the self-serving, me-first nature of mankind alone renders such a position suspect, problematic, and questionable at the very least. The work of God breaking through into the world and miraculously transforming the hearts and daily lives of people in ways that cannot be explained and exceeds our imagination are evident to those with eyes to see.

God made us to know Him, and in so doing, honor Him, love Him, depend on Him, and trust Him with the details of our personal, daily lives. Surely, we've all had small (some bigger than others) indications of God working redemptively behind the scenes, but most experiences remain inadequate and less than a fully satisfying peek into eternity and the sovereignty of God, and open to personal bias and interpretations — that is, attempts to fit God into a particular box.

We've seen the night sky filled nightly with majestic stars and galaxies too numerous to count, all testifying to the greatness and splendor of God. With the passing of every season, we've observed the wonder of God's ability to consistently paint the beauty of a sunset on a cool, crisp autumn day. We've noted the distant horizon with the rising of the sun every morning, shouting the promise of a new day. We've observed the awesome power of nature and a glimpse of the God who created it all — the crashing of the ocean waves, the strength and persistence of the wind, and the majestic mountain peaks colored white with snow reaching high into the sky. Beautiful — every bit of it, just beautiful. God's fingerprints are all over the universe. Impressive, but it's not enough.

We've witnessed the miracle and marvel of birth and heard the cries and laughter of a precious child, filled with wonder and the potential and promise of a life yet to be lived. We've seen Picasso and Rembrandt, listened to Mozart and the Beach Boys, and readily recognize the creative genius of a God so big, so glorious, so majestic and magnificent, it boggles the imagination. This is the God Who lives and works outside the box, the One who fills my life with song, and with every stroke of His divine brush, paints my life with spectacular grandeur, purpose, and meaning. Despite all the beauty and splendor of it all, it still remains little more than a cursory, though important, view of the divine. The spiritual ability of flesh and blood to see God is restricted, leaving us wanting and needing more to discover this side of eternity. For now, we see God *"piece by piece"* (cf. I Corinthians 13:9),[11] but *"in the face of Jesus Christ we best see the glory of God."*[12]

I want more intimacy with God, a deeper relationship with Him. I want to gaze deeper into His eyes, to gain more understanding, more vision, more truth to expand my limited knowledge of Him and the world around me. On occasion, I need to *"touch the fringe of his robe"* (Matthew 9:20, NLT).

Nothing has changed through the centuries from the Garden of Eden onward. We continue to amass an impressive array of information. Knowledge we got. We've seen the growth of various philosophical and religious systems from New Age doctrine to the New Atheism and from Augustine's *Confessions* to Nietzsche's "God is dead," as well as the adoption of post-modern and post-truth thinking — all steadily on the rise and expanding. The choices before us are astounding. The abundance of scientific data currently available, the growth of medical treatment options, and the development of modern machinery to meet nearly every conceivable, creaturely comfort we can think of (electric toothbrushes, vibrating chairs, prepared meals delivered to our front door, motorized wheelchairs, etc.) are increasing at a staggering rate. It is truly remarkable. The advancement of technology and the internet (computers, cell phones, Alexa, trips to the moon and back, driverless cars, Facebook, Twitter, Snapchat, etc.) are overwhelming, yet the modern world with its impressive array of accumulated knowledge and information and technological wizardry seems to know even less about God than its ancestors.

An ordained pastor and member of the U.S. House of Representatives opened the 117th Congress of the United States in prayer and closed his petition appealing to "the name of the monotheistic (Hindu) God, Brahma, and gods known by many names by many different faiths." Apparently, he was covering all his religious, ecumenical bases, not wanting to leave any potential god out of the mix. He then ended his prayer with "Amen and a-woman"[13] — another indication that a seminary degree is no guarantee of one's ability and willingness to grasp, endorse, and apply orthodox, historical Christian doctrine about God to everyday life. Though the congressman tried to play off his remarks as an attempt at humor, it was undoubtedly a poor joke. The French author and playwright Alexandre Dumas fils (1824–1895) wrote, "One thing that humbles me deeply is to see that human genius has its limits while human stupidity does not."[14] I think the old boy was on to something. Obviously, formal theological and pastoral training is not a sure pathway to acquiring a genuine, working knowledge of the true God. You might be tempted to think otherwise.

One clergy member from a major denomination told me he believed that when Jesus said to Nicodemus, *"You must be born again"* (John 3:7), he was talking and teaching about reincarnation, a concept completely foreign to Christianity and incompatible with historic orthodoxy. I was stunned by his ignorance, shocked by his ineptness to handle the Scriptures well, and angered by his failure to fulfill his responsibility as a shepherd of the sheep and lead his people toward Christ and nowhere else. He was guilty of speaking *"falsehood"* and misleading God's people" (cf. Ezekiel 13:8, 10), a serious indictment (not uncommon today) which ultimately brings divine judgment. A most unpleasant prospect.

Today, evil is but a social construct and little more. Satan is no longer viewed as a real adversary who wreaks havoc in the world and comes *"only to steal, and kill, and destroy"* (John 10:10) the lives of people. Righteous (right) living ceases to be clearly defined or determined within the context of daily life. Biblical standards have been reinterpreted to appease a secular crowd where everyone is left to do what is *"right in his own eyes"* (Judges 21:25). The faith once delivered to the saints is under attack (cf. Jude 3). Traditional marriage is discarded. Gender and identity issues are unclear and border on lunacy. The sanctity of life is aborted. The foundational beliefs of the church have been redefined apart from biblical revelation. The inspiration and authority of the Scriptures are no longer accepted and believed to be unimportant. In short, the reality of God is nowhere to be found. The church has gone missing from the world, and the world has missed the relevance of the church and the truth of Who God is, what He is like, and what truly matters. God has effectively been shoved into a variety of man-made theological and philosophical boxes, and He doesn't fit any of them outside the pages of the Bible and the Person and character of Christ.

In a word, God has been successfully crowded out of our daily lives, educational institutions, and some of our churches where orthodox Christianity has been tossed out and theological and behavioral madness reigns. Neither God or His Word are revered or recognizable in the current cancel-culture environment where there is virtually no limit to the boxes we can construct to put God in. We suffer from intellectual confusion and spiritual shortsightedness.

Paul reinforced our ignorance of divinity when he wrote to young Timothy that God *"alone possesses immortality and dwells in unapproachable light* [figure that out], *whom no man has seen or can see"* (I Timothy 6:16, NLT) — an immense problem for all humankind because gaining a true understanding of God is critically important and foundational to our well-being in this life and the life to come.

Our most intimate knowledge of God (how we view Him) drives our decisions and defines our motives, and in turn influences our behavior, either good or bad. Lauren Mitchell, author of *Steadfast* (a devotional book about prayer and King David's dependence upon his heavenly Father), asked God for one word that she could carry with her through the days and months of 2020. The word was "believe." Surprisingly, the same word was given her for 2021. She wrote (Facebook, Jan 15, 2021):

> *Satan is most threatened by our complete belief in God, because deception is his forte. If we are unflinchingly believing the truth about God, Satan runs out of options. The root of any unbelief is always a lie (about God) that we are actively believing (with devasting consequences).*

The Apostle Paul fervently prayed that God might grant first-century believers (and the rest of us) the necessary *"spiritual wisdom and insight…(to) grow in (the) knowledge of God"* (Ephesians 1:17, NLT). We desperately need it. Paul believed it important to the health and well-being of both saint and sinner alike, and so he intervened on our behalf, pleading with God to give us the wherewithal, the means to do what we could not and cannot possibly do for ourselves without assistance from above, and that is:

> **Ephesians 3:18–19, ESV** – *[to] comprehend [grasp, seize, truly understand] with all the saints what is the breadth and length and height and depth, and to know the love of Christ that surpasses knowledge, that you may be filled with all the fullness of God.*

Knowing the reality of the love of God will change your perspective about yourself and the manner in which you are living out your daily life.

On the night of April 14, 1912, off the coast of Newfoundland in the icy North Atlantic seas, the "unsinkable" Titanic struck an iceberg. The captain had boasted earlier that, "Even God himself cannot sink the *Titanic*." But a hundred and sixty minutes of terror later, the luxury liner went down. The following day the headlines read: "1500 Persons Sink to a Watery Grave." Legend has it that amidst passenger panic and hysteria the ship's orchestra was heard playing on deck. It was a courageous effort to calm, comfort, and encourage the hearts of drowning men and women. Carlos F. Hurd, a thirty-six-year-old reporter from the *St. Louis Post-Dispatch*, was on the *Carpathia* that tragic night as it sailed to the rescue of survivors. He reported the following, gleaned from eyewitness accounts.

> *As the screams in the water multiplied, another sound was heard, strong and clear at first, then fainter in the distance. It was the melody of the hymn "Nearer, My God, to Thee," played by the string orchestra in the dining saloon. Some of those on the water started to sing the words, but grew silent as they realized that for the men who played, the music was a sacrament soon to be*

> *consummated by death. The serene strains of the hymn and the frantic cries of the dying blended in a symphony of sorrow.*[15]

I can assure you that there was no boxing God in that night. They wanted the "Real Thing." Me, too. They wanted to find God. They wanted to pursue Him, the One they knew was able to rescue them, to sustain them in life and death. A good move when the reality of death and the nearness of eternity are approaching.

When God is *"near,"* when you recognize that the Creator-God Who made heaven and earth has a firm hold on your life, you settle down, and life no longer looks so foreboding, out of control, and hopeless (cf. Philippians 4:4–7). James wrote, *"Come* [imperative] *close to God* [and do it now, immediately without delay], *and God will come close to you"* (James 4:8, NLT). That's a fact. The more you discover the truth about God, the easier the decision to jump in the "lifeboat" with Him and trust Him to take you back to your earthly home or deliver you safely to your heavenly mansion. Either works for me. "By waters still, o'er troubled sea, Still 'tis His hand that leadeth me."[16]

Don't box God in. He is more than you think.

---

**II Peter 3:18, NIV** – *"But grow in the grace and knowledge of our Lord and Savior Jesus Christ. To him be glory both now and forever! Amen."*

> *"Our best chance of finding God is to look in the place where we left him."*[1]
>
> —Meister Eckhart
> (Dominican theologian and writer, 1260-1327/28)

# 4

# "ARE YOU GUYS READY? LET'S ROLL!"

> —The last words spoken by Todd Beamer
> aboard the hijacked United Airlines Flight 93
> September 11, 2001

I had just concluded a funeral service during which I spoke fervently of the hope we have in Christ, particularly in the face of death. I spoke of the cross, God's mercy and forgiveness, redemption, eternity, and Heaven. I was (and still am) convinced of the reality of the resurrection and the implications for the future of every believer. Surprisingly, the funeral director pulled me aside following the service and privately asked me a pointed question. I was caught off guard and a bit shocked by his inquiry, considering the number of funerals he had directed over his professional career and because he had been an active member in a local church for many years.

He asked disparagingly, "Do you really believe all those things you were saying?"

I could see the pain in his eyes. He had recently buried a close family member and was still mourning. It was an honest question, and so I answered him the best I could.

"Of course, I do. What else is there? Where else do we go for help and hope in times like these? If there is no truth to the gospel, then once my feet hit the grave, there is nothing else. It's over and anything I might have done, achieved, or experienced (the good stuff and the tough stuff) during my days on planet earth mean nothing. And that's unacceptable. There must be more to life than the average seventy trips around the sun, or you and I are wasting our time here; and we are *"of all men most to be pitied"* (cf. I Corinthians 15:14, 17, 19).

I could tell that he wasn't convinced. Here was a man who had spent his entire adult life serving the church and the community and the needs of fearful, hurting people looking for hope and comfort in the face of humanity's greatest and fiercest enemy. He had none to give. Death arrived at his own front door, and he had no answers. No confidence. No comfort. No faith. No fight left in him. He had lost touch with God, at least for the moment. Lost sight of the God of eternity and forgotten the gospel — that the lives of men and women redeemed by the grace of God, shown at the cross, are forever reconciled to God. *"He who believes in Me,"* Jesus said, *"shall live even if he dies"* (John 11:25). Death has no ultimate victory, no final say, particularly in the case of those who trust Christ during their lifetime for the forgiveness of their sins and the welfare of their eternal soul. Heaven is surely secured for the redeemed. That's the truth of the gospel, plain and simple. Instead, the man's heart was filled with ambiguity about life, death, and eternity, and he struggled with indecision regarding the veracity of God's Word. Consequently, he was discouraged and distraught, unsure of anything, except the certainty of the funeral (which he had witnessed hundreds of times over the years). He was convinced of one thing only — once the lid was closed, no corpse had ever climbed out of a coffin, at least not in his presence. He had become a temporary skeptic who thought and lived like an agnostic. Death overwhelmed him and left the man with a host of doubts and questions. The grave seemed so final, so hapless, so hopeless. Blinded in the darkness that engulfed his mind and overwhelmed his heart, it had been a long time since he had "seen" God. He needed a fresh new hope to sustain him.

In 64 AD, the Apostle Peter wrote to suffering, persecuted Christians, who lived through the brutal reign of Nero, a decadent and unpopular emperor, who 'fiddled' while his city burned before his very eyes and then blamed followers of Christ for the tragedy. Christians had seen enough death in their lifetime, experienced enough hardship, and shed enough tears for God to collect and fill His *"bottle"* (Psalm 56:8). Peter reassured them. *"And the God of all grace, who called you to his eternal glory in Christ, after you have suffered a little while, will himself restore you and make you strong, firm and steadfast"* (I Peter 5:10, NIV). Words of hope and comfort. When it's too dark for me to see God, there is a God who sees me, Who will reach out, find me (when I can't seem to find Him), and meet me in the shadows of trial and trouble to show me the way out of my misery and *"restore to me the joy of Thy salvation"* (Psalm 51:12).

As I stood in the office of that heartbroken man listening to the cry of his heart, I was reminded of a comment attributed to H.G. Wells: "If there is no God, nothing matters. If there is a God, nothing else matters."[2] Apart from God and a relationship with Him, there is no reason or much value for putting on my pants in the morning (other than maybe modesty, social pressure and practice, and covering up this old wrinkled, flabby, worn-out body), and heading out the door. For what? To do what? To what end?

It did not take Solomon long to learn that lesson, as well — there is no real, deep, lasting *"enjoyment* (in life) *without Him* (God)*"* (Ecclesiastes 2:25). On his knees before the altar of the Lord *"with his hands spread toward heaven,"* (cf. I Kings 8:54), Solomon summarized his life experience in a prayer for his people, wanting them to know how to prosper in the coming years: *"Let your heart therefore be wholly true to the Lord our God, walking in his statutes and keeping his commandments"* (I Kings 8:61). In contrast, the results of living for self, apart from knowing and pursuing God Himself, leaves a man or woman short on life's purpose, ultimately producing a shallow existence. A pointless world. Might as well stay in bed, pull down the shades and the covers up, and quit on life, or at the very least, eat all the cheeseburgers and fries you can stomach, get your cholesterol levels up, clog all those arteries, and drink all the whiskey and Michelob you want, *"for tomorrow we die"* (I Corinthians 15:32). One might as well "party hearty," a viable alternative for many, since life serves no real purpose and ends in the cemetery anyway. And then what? A hangover? That's it? Nothing more? It all seems so trivial and absurd.

In the 1989 movie *Dead Poets Society*, John Keating, an English professor (played by Robin Williams), teaching at Welton Academy, a prestigious all-boys preparatory school, told his students to "seize the day because we are food for worms, lads. Because believe it or not, each and every one of us in this room is one day going to stop breathing, turn cold and die."[3] The message was/is clear. Go do what you want to do. Go where you want to go, while you can. Self-indulgence and self-gratification is your highest goal. Fill life with what feels good and right to you. Seek pleasure and happiness above all. The opportunity passes quickly. No moral obligation or purpose is necessary. Grab all the gusto in life you can manage, because in the end, "food for worms" will be your final legacy. Nothing more. Nothing else. A rather bleak prospect and hopeless approach to daily living. We need to look for something better and something more.

Theologian Paul Tillich spoke of the "threat of non-being" as a source of anxiety, where at the end of some seventy years or so, one simply ceases to exist, and nothing is of any substantial consequence or worth. Frankly, that's a devasting, disturbing thought — humanity (and that includes you and me) doomed and condemned to be buried under six feet of dirt, and that's it, having lived out our days and died without any ultimate meaning or significance.[4] We soon end our lives much like Porky Pig, who stammered at the end of every cartoon I watched as a kid, "And that's all folks!" It's over. No more. Nothing else to say or do. No purpose for having lived. No real value to our individual stories. Nothing of genuine importance.

No, thank you! Not interested in simply going through the motions of a daily routine with no real rhyme or reason in sight, no matter how popular, brilliant or lofty it may seem at the moment! Searching for God and the best He has in store for me is how I want to spend my days. Everything else pales in comparison.

In June 2005, Steve Kroft of 60 Minutes interviewed Tom Brady, the celebrated quarterback for the New England Patriots. Kroft asked Brady what effect all his success has had on him. Brady replied:

> *Why do I have three [now six] Super Bowl rings and still think there's something greater out there for me? I mean…I reached my goal, my dream, my life…God, it's gotta be more than this. I mean, this can't be what it's all cracked up to be. I mean, I've done it. I'm twenty-seven. And what else is there for me?*[5]

An admission of dissatisfaction and discontent from the lips of one of the most highly decorated and truly successful players ever to put on a helmet and pads. "This can't be all" is a common tale told among men, when God is not in the picture. Jesus taught that God is the ground, the "rock" (cf. Matthew 7:24–27) upon which a "wise man" must build a life that truly counts. Nothing else will do because God and God alone is the answer to "non-being," to the meaninglessness that so many fear and experience.

Dorothy Sayers, the Christian humanist and writer, warns of:

> *the sin which believes in nothing, cares for nothing, seeks to know nothing, interferes with nothing, enjoys nothing, loves nothing, hates nothing, finds purpose in nothing, lives for nothing, and only remains alive because there is nothing it would die for.*[6]

Carl Sagan, the controversial planetary scientist, launched the thirteen-part TV series "Cosmos" in 1980 with these words: "The

Cosmos is all there is, all there was, and all there ever will be."[7] Another rather depressing conviction, the implications of which are staggering and disheartening — the sin of living for nothing. We had better search for something more and commit to something greater.

We do have, however, another path to consider, a better approach to daily life, another more constructive and productive way to face the day — living experientially, practically, and personally in light of the knowledge of God. In the end, a life based on intimacy with God brings fullness of life, immeasurable love and acceptance, the removal of guilt for past failures and sins (and there are plenty of those), real hope in a tragic and fallen world, and a deep sense of satisfaction day by day while serving the King and the eternal interests of His kingdom. But I first need to see God as He is, not like I want Him to be if the best results for daily living are to be realized.

Elijah, the Old Testament prophet, did just that. He had encountered God at the lowest and highest points of his career. He met God in a cave and at the top of a mountain; both experiences dramatically altered the course of his life. Such experiences always do.

Elijah had the reputation of being the *"troubler of Israel"* (I Kings 18:17), a title and role I think he relished, though at times the prophet didn't seem all that tough. He *"ran for his life…into the wilderness"* (I Kings 19:3–4) with his tail between his legs to hide from the likes of Ahab and Jezebel, depressed, disheartened, wanting to die (v. 4), and unsure of what would come of his life if he stuck around to face another day. But amidst his self-pity and uncertainty, he found the Person and power of God to take on life with a holy abandonment, motivated and encouraged by God to consider the significance of his divine mission. Subsequently, God moved with precision and invaded the man's day-to-day world, disrupted Elijah's plans (He seems to do that a lot in my life, as well), and met him *"by the brook Cherith."* For starters, God served him supper for his physical needs, encouraged his downtrodden heart, lifted his anxious spirit, and then sent him down a path with a clear set of directions for the journey ahead. Elijah, whose name means, *"My God is power,"* discovered the *"mighty One of Israel — Elohim,"* and it made a tremendous difference in his life and ministry. The knowledge of God empowered him and readied him for anything the day might bring. From spineless to fearless. From coward to gutsy. He stood tall, having been called by God to "man up!" He was under divine orders to pick a fight with a belligerent, obstinate bunch of religious yahoos (that's the Hebrew word for bonehead) and challenge them to a contest of spiritual wit and brawn — "winner take all." He was outmanned 850 to 1, but no matter. He had met with God prior to the confrontation (the most important decision he ever made) and came away from that encounter knowing that God was calling the shots and He alone would decide the outcome of the battle that would carry the prophet to triumph amidst trial and trouble. The end had already been determined — the sovereignty of God would soon be on display for all to see as God sent down fire from heaven to consume the sacrifice drenched with water that was lying on an altar.

Elijah's success was intricately tied to how well and how clearly he saw and trusted God. And so it is for the rest of us. He was victorious precisely because God initiated contact with a desperate man who needed to hear from heaven (cf. I Kings 18:36). Os Guinness wrote:

> *You cannot find God without God. We cannot reach God without God. We cannot satisfy God without God — which is another way of saying that our seeking will always fall short unless God's grace initiates the search and unless God's call draws us to him and completes the search.*[8]

From the beginning of time, God has made (and continues to make) the first move. Driven by a love so exceedingly deep and a plan so incomprehensibly perfect, God pursued a fallen humanity from the very start. He had to. Adam and Eve were too busy running away to a place (any place) that would hide their guilt and shame. They fled from the very presence of God, trying to make it on their own (sounds familiar), ignoring God's warnings and directives, and wholly resisting any interference from Him in their personal lives. Neither God, nor anyone else for that matter, was/is going to tell them (or me) what to do, though God's Word and will were/are designed for their (and my) well-being and success. Again, not much has changed. The whole sorry scenario continues to this day. We are still hiding from God, and He is still looking to connect with you and me, bridge the gap between Heaven and earth, reconcile our differences, close the distance between us, and build a solid love relationship with all men and women that will outlast eternity.

The results of Elijah having met with God was nothing short of spectacular. A dramatic and immediate transformation took place — the freedom to become the man God created him and called him to be. The parallel to our own personal, daily lives is unmistakable. The same thing happens the day we meet and experience God. Let the search continue in earnest. "Let's roll!"

Elijah emerged from that dark cave a different man (and you will, too) — energized, confident, sure of himself, and more importantly, sure of God. At the deepest of levels, he had come to know *"the Lord of hosts."* No longer was he reluctant or fearful to act. He was a man who had met God (cf. I Kings 18:15), heard Him speak into his life, and then boldly stepped forward to carry out God's orders for the day and bring the full weight of the authority and power of God to bear on every detail of daily living. *"If the Lord is God, then follow Him!"* A principle Elijah endorsed and validated. The people who climbed Mt. Carmel that fateful day would witness and know God as an experiential reality, not just as a set of cold theological dictums and religious beliefs. God was for real!

Elijah had an honest, no-holds-barred relationship with God — personal, individual, and specific (I could use some of that myself). In short, he and God were on speaking terms (a solid objective for any person), and subsequently, it paid big dividends in the prophet's life — a little hutzpah (if you will), the mettle to stand courageously for the truth and confront and counter the religious and political leaders of his day, challenge the current culture with a better way to live, and challenge every life standard and social norm contrary to God's Word, including every *"empty philosophy* (Colossians 2:8, NLT), and popular religious doctrine — *"every lofty thing raised up against the knowledge of God"* (II Corinthians 10:5). It was a battle waged over the supremacy of ideas and the truth about the reality and authority of God. We are fighting the same battles today, and that is the very reason why we must personally experience God, search Him out, and draw close to Him if we are to hold our own and thrive in this troublesome world.

Following the May 2021 shootings, where nine people were shot and killed at a rail yard in San Jose, California, Archbishop Paul S. Coakley, chairman of the United States Conference of Catholic Bishops Committee on Domestic Justice and Human Development, assessed the tragedy and concluded that something is "fundamentally broken in our society."[9] He is right on target, but the solution is not simply legislation nor education to curb the violence and indifference toward human life which he suggested, though each has their place in addressing the problem. However, neither approach will adequately reach the heart of man.

What will work is to "get out of the cave," find, know, and follow hard after God. He is the ultimate solution for a troubled soul. The search for God in Christ and His Word must take place, and quickly. It cannot wait, for when the truth is uncovered and applied to the "inner man," society will change because men and women will *"no longer be conformed to this world, but… transformed"* (Romans 12:2) to reflect the character, motives, and actions of God, and as *"imitators of God"* (Ephesians 5:1), walk in love, just as Christ did. The results will be self-evident — people living as God intended in faith, hope, peace, joy, love and power. The task is plain. Seek the truth, weigh out the evidence (and there is plenty of it), and get on with discovering who God is and what He requires. "Let's roll!"

In the 1989 classic, *Indiana Jones and the Last Crusade*, Walter Donovan, an antiquities dealer who had allied himself with the Nazis, was in search of the Holy Grail "that gives everlasting life." He found the Grail in the Temple of the Sun guarded by a single knight who had stood his post for the last seven hundred years. The Grail was seated on a large table with a multitude of other chalices and cups. Donovan was bewildered and perplexed. He hadn't known, nor could he recognize, the identity of the true Grail. And so he asks, "Which one is it?"

"You must choose," the knight replied, "but choose wisely, as the true grail will bring you life; the false grail will take it from you."

Donovan surveyed the table, and with a little help from an accomplice, he made his choice with confidence, picking it up in his hands and lifting it toward the heavens. "It's more beautiful than I ever imagined" he declared, "Certainly, this is the cup of the King of kings." He selected an exquisite gold chalice decorated with fine jewels. It looked good, felt right in his hands, and so he drank from the cup to test its authenticity, fully expecting his personal life to profit and gain. That's what he wanted. That was what he believed. But the cup was a fraud, a fake. In the end, he gained nothing and lost everything. The cup didn't work as expected (false gods don't either, promising the world on a golden platter, but delivering so much less), and it cost him dearly. The results were catastrophic. His body began to disintegrate and crumble into dust. His life was lost, destroyed by the choices he made. The knight, who had watch the entire, tragic event unfold, drew his final conclusion, "He chose poorly."[10]

May God give us eyes to see more clearly, to know Him better, to readily recognize Him, and to wisely choose Him as the only true God, worthy of our full devotion, affection, and worship. To do otherwise will most certainly end in calamity and misfortune.

In a world that boasts a multiplicity of gods, from the idolatry of man himself to more than 3,000 Hindu deities and a plethora of other historical and modern religious and philosophical systems too numerous to count, you cannot remain neutral in this pursuit. It's too important to your own well-being — not only now, but over the long haul. The eternal state of your soul and the quality of your daily experiences are on the line. You must decide. I must decide. Look. Examine. Investigate. Conclude. Then act in concert with your convictions. Don't *"hesitate...If the Lord is God, follow Him"* (I Kings 18:21). If not, go your own way and serve one of the many other gods out there clamoring for your attention and affection. But make no mistake. You will serve somebody or something — self, pride, esteem, position, power, intellect, whatever the work of your own hands can construct and your own imagination can conceive. A multiplicity of gods await to take the willing follower down any number of paths going nowhere and forming a vast array of muddled ideas and purpose. C.S. Lewis said:

> *All that we call human history — money, poverty, ambition, war, prostitution, classes, empires, slavery — [is] the long terrible story of man trying to find something other than God which will make him happy.*[11]

That "something" does not exist. It never has. Nothing can fill our deepest longings other than God. So, from which cup will you drink? A cup made of "fool's gold" or the cup of a Carpenter named Jesus? The choice you make will be the most important decision you will ever make in life. Find God, and you find your purpose and calling. Find God, and you find your life's path — a worthwhile, productive, meaningful adventure, a journey with God leading you every step of the way. *"Don't bargain with God. Be direct. Ask for what you need. This isn't a cat-and-mouse, hide-and-seek game we're in"* (Matthew 7:7, MSG). The prescription for living successfully in this world is no secret. *"If the Lord is God, follow Him."* Even the mighty Elijah who was later seen running scared and hiding in a cave needed reminding: Get out of there!

### Let's Roll!

*"What are you doing here, Elijah?" (I Kings 19:9, 13).*
*A disturbing question for every servant and follower of God.*
*Penetrating,*

*Probing,*
*Prying,*
*Deep into the crevices of a troubled soul.*
*A soul that often*
*Wallows in self-pity;*
*Whines about the tough days;*
*Wishes for something better, something different;*
*Wonders whether anything really matters.*
*Like so many, Elijah ran from life.*
*Afraid.*
*Terrified.*
*Cowering before an enemy hell-bent on destroying him.*
*A story common among flesh and blood...An all-too-familiar scene.*
*Loss of fervency.*
*Loss of focus.*
*Loss of faith.*
*In the miraculous,*
*In the mystery of the Divine,*
*In the mission.*
*The prophet lost much. Trials and hardships can do that.*
*Predictably, a journey to the "wilderness" (I Kings 19:4) will often follow.*
*Dry,*
*Barren,*
*Lonely days, which end in a dark, cold cave.*
*Distracted from my tasks.*
*Demoralized by my thoughts.*
*Depressed about my future.*
*Prepared to quit. Willing to*
*Walk out on God,*
*Walk out on my calling,*
*Walk out on myself.*
*Elijah had come to the end.*

*"Enough!" he cried.*
*"No more!"*
*Been there myself.*
*But there is more.*
*There is hope.*
*There is an answer for such despair and dismay…*
*The simple, yet profound, instructions of God for everyday life.*
*His Word,*
*His will,*
*Done His way.*
*In the quiet voice of the divine,*
*In the gentle whisper of the wind,*
*In the rustling of the pages of Scripture*
*the Spirit of God speaks…again and again.*
*"Are you guys ready? Let's roll!"*
*"Wonderful words of life," wrote the hymn writer.*
*There is no other place to go to calm an anxious soul.*
*God is not silent. He never is.*
*"Go forth…and STAND on the mountain before the Lord"*
*(I Kings 19:11) is what God told Elijah.*
*A good place for Him (and me) to be: "Before the Lord."*
*Standing erect, head up, ready to*
*Move as God directs.*
*Act as He wills.*
*Change what He desires to change.*
*Nothing more.*
*Nothing less.*
*The message is clear and concise for those of us who have lived*
*too long in "a cave."*
*That dark, foreboding place of*
*Personal failure,*
*Destroyed marriages,*
*Moral lapses,*
*Brokenness,*

*Wayward kids,*
*Hopelessness,*
*Lost opportunities,*
*Doubts and fears.*
*Death and disease.*
*Whatever...*
*The "word of God came to him" (I Kings 19:9),*
*And it comes to me, too.*
*A good word.*
*A motivating word.*
*A transforming word.*
*A powerful word.*
*"Get up!*
*Get out!*
*And get on with life!"*
*Remember!*
*Self-pity is much too costly. It*
*Depletes courage,*
*Voids the future,*
*Lowers resolve,*
*Lessens self-worth,*
*Drains the soul.*
*But the Word of the Lord stands forever.*
*His promises are sure. His plans are perfect,*
*"Restoring the soul,"*
*"Making wise the simple,"*
*"Rejoicing the heart"*
*Enlightening the eyes" (Psalm 19:7–9).*
*"Go forth" (I Kings 19:15)!*
*Don't wait.*
*Seek God.*
*Open His Book!*
*Hear "the word of the Lord" (I Kings 19:9). And you will find*

*Healing for a wounded heart,*
*Peace for an anxious, fearful spirit,*
*Direction for misguided thinking.*
*Take some spiritual nourishment.*
*Eat the Bread of Life…the revelation of God.*
*Drink "living water" (I Kings 19:6, John 7:37–38), the Spirit of God.*
*Get your divine orders.*
*The sure promises of God's Word.*
*"WHAT ARE YOU DOING HERE, ELIJAH?"*
*What am I doing here?*
*Get back in the fight.*
*Refreshed by the power of God.*
*Run from the cave!*
*"Go!"*
*"Get up!*
*Get out!*
*Get on with life!"*
*No wallowing.*
*No whining.*
*No wishing things should be better.*
*Enough of that!*
*GET OUT OF THE CAVE!*
*Find God.*
*"Are you guys ready? Let's roll."*

(Todd Beamer, Flight 93, 9/11)
—Sandy

*"The deeper we get into reality, the more numerous will be the questions we cannot answer."*

— Friedrich Von Hugel,
author and theologian (1852–1925)

# 5

# THE MYSTERY OF GOD

Howard Hendricks (*Living by the Book,* Moody Publishers 2007) told of a research scientist who studied the characteristics of a flea. He wanted to know just what this flea was capable of doing…how it functioned, how it moved, just how strong it was. So he picked it up and plucked off one leg, set it back down on the lab table, and told it to jump. The flea complied. The scientist took the experiment a little further and plucked off another leg and again commanded the flea to jump. To the surprise of the researcher, the flea jumped again. This continued until the sixth and final leg was torn from the body of the flea. Once more, the scientist yelled, "Jump." But the flea lay still on the table, unmoving. The scientist raised his voice a bit higher, "Jump!" No response. No change. One more time, he screamed louder than before, "JUMP!" Still nothing. The flea remained motionless. The scientist thought for a few moments then took out his notebook to record his observations: "When you remove the legs from a flea," he wrote, "it loses its sense of hearing and is no longer able to hear commands and respond in any significant manner."¹ So often, I've missed the obvious in my search for God and have drawn the wrong conclusions about Him.

God is and remains a mystery. *"Truly, You are a God who hides Himself, O God of Israel, Savior"* (Isaiah 45:15, AMP). That makes Him tough to recognize and find, unless of course, He willingly steps out of the shadows of obscurity and makes Himself visible to the human heart, which by the way, He has already done. As we've seen, God defies being put into a theological box for human consumption or manipulation and doctrinal convenience. *Incomprehensible* is the word theologians use to describe what little we know about the Creator of the universe, Who is *"before all things, and in Him all things hold together"* (Colossians 1:17). Let that rattle around in your brain for just a bit. Words are obviously insufficient to explain the depths of divinity. Language is inadequate. Culture is of no help. The ideas of philosophers are no better. Reason is of little use here, especially when attempting to define and understand the Godhead. Unsurprisingly, we find ourselves hard-pressed to figure out God. I've tried. It doesn't work so well, and I've been left wanting in my efforts, dissatisfied, confused, and wondering at times if God is just too far away to get a good look, too distant for me to connect with, and/or too mysterious for me to intellectually untangle or make sense of. "For of what use is existence to the creature, if it cannot know its Maker."²

After the publication of his book *The God Delusion*, outspoken atheist and Oxford professor Richard Dawkins sat down with Christian scientist Francis Collins and the editors of *TIME* magazine to debate the origins of the universe and the idea of God as "a supernatural, intelligent designer." At the end of the debate, Dawkins concluded:

> *My mind is not closed [to the idea of God]…My mind is open to the most wonderful range of future possibilities, which I cannot even dream about, nor can you, nor can anybody else…If there is a God, it's going to be a whole lot bigger and a whole lot more*

> *incomprehensible than anything that any theologian of any religion has ever proposed.*[3]

Some of the world's greatest minds are powerless to probe the depths of God and His existence, His being, or His character, at least not without some significant help. There are, however, sufficient "clues," suggested C. S. Lewis (the presence of love and goodness in the world, a universal moral law of right and wrong, the demand for justice, the historical evidence for Jesus, the structure of the world and the precision of the universe, etc.)[4] that make the notion of the existence of God, the Designer and Creator of all, a reasonable and rational choice.

Art Linkletter saw a small boy drawing a picture. He inquired, "What are you drawing?" The boy replied, "A picture of God." Linkletter told the youngster that no one knows what God looks like, to which the boy confidently responded, "They will when I get through."[5] The reality of God and His character can be clearly seen in the recorded stories and testimonies of those who have walked the streets of the ancient world, as well as those of every generation who have encountered and experienced a touch from God in their personal daily lives.

Nik Ripken, a twenty-five-year missionary veteran, was listening to a group of Ukrainian believers share their personal stories of prison, persecution, and God's faithfulness in seeing them through those dark, difficult days. The testimonies were extraordinary, powerful, convincing, and insightful. Ripken said, "I just don't understand why you haven't collected these stories in a book? Believers around the world ought to hear what you have been telling me today…(They are) inspiring." One older, experienced pastor stepped forward, looked Ripken in the eye and asked,

> *Son, when did you stop reading your Bible? [That cuts deep]. All of our stories are in the Bible. God has already written them down. Why would we bother writing books to tell our stories when*

> *God has already told His story. If you would just read the Bible, you would see that our stories are there.*[6]

Good point. If I would just read the Bible more consistently and deeply, I would find a God the likes of whom I had never known or imagined existed. His story is there in the chronicled events of history and in the lives of everyday people.

If the truth be told, we have missed God along the way, though His footprints are everywhere. Actually, we've never truly understood ourselves let alone God. We are a bundle of paradoxes, a living contradiction (love and hate, faithful and disloyal, patient and impatient, kind and spiteful, etc.) unable to fully clarify the purpose and meaning of life and death, nor grasp the beginning of the cosmos and its Architect. Let's face it. Nobody was there but God Himself when His imagination was let loose to form galaxies too many to count. Philosophers and scientists have tried for centuries to figure this stuff out but remain stymied, falling short and failing to come to grips with the question of the Creator of the universe and the deep character of a holy God. Those particulars escape me as well. If I could fully comprehend, define, and make sense (and I can't) of the first four words of the Bible — *"In the beginning, God…,"* you might consider falling at my feet and calling me "God" — *Elohim*, the infinite, all-powerful Lord of the ages (and we all know that's not happening). So apparently, you and I have to look elsewhere and set out to find and recognize the Person and work of God in my personal life and in the world at large.

Finite beings are short on grasping infinity. What we think of God remains clouded in ambiguity and encased within our own self-serving ideas and often thoughtless opinions. Simply put, we have no accurate definitions of the divine nor do we possess a clear, unobstructed understanding or view of who He is in His fullness, where to find Him, and what He truly desires from us all. Humanity has always surrounded itself with a plethora of gods, none of whom makes much sense to flesh and blood.

Zophar the Naamathite challenged Job, who was trying to understand the trouble he was in and where God might fit into the picture. *"Can you discover the depths of God? Can you discover the limits of the Almighty?"* he asked (Job 11:7). The question is rhetorical. It demands a firm, "No, I can't!" *"The thunder of (God's) mighty power"* (Job 26:14) is beyond human comprehension. In fact, it strikes fear in each of us. It should. It is but a hint of God's omnipotence. The best Elihu (another of Job's friends with a big mouth) could say was that he *"fetched (his) knowledge (of God) from afar"* (Job 36:3). And *"afar"* is an accurate depiction of our inadequacies and theological shortsightedness. Elihu spoke the truth. The extent of our collective knowledge about God and God's ways are not terribly impressive. *"God is exalted, and we do not know Him"* (Job 36:26). But we need too, and we must.

In September 1982, my wife and I attended the Billy Graham School of Evangelism in Boston. S.M. Lockridge, that great preacher of another generation, gave the keynote address (which I will not ever forget) before some eighteen hundred pastors and wives. He told the story of preaching in Detroit at a meeting where he had made the comment that "God came from nowhere," and concluded that this was both "theologically correct and biblically sound…"

A man approached him afterwards and challenged him. "Preacher, let's be reasonable_about this thing. You were up there tonight (saying that) God came from nowhere, and that doesn't make sense. Let's be reasonable about it." Dr. Lockridge shared his response to the man's objections.

*All right. If you want to be reasonable about it, the reason God came from nowhere, there wasn't any place for Him to come from. And coming from nowhere, He stood on nothing. The reason he had to stand on nothing, there was nowhere for Him to stand. And standing on nothing, He reached out where there was nowhere to reach and caught something when there was nothing to catch and hung something on nothing and told it stay there (Job 26 and 27). And standing on nothing, He took the hammer*

> *of His own will, and He struck the anvil of His omnipotence (unlimited power), and sparks flew therefrom. And He caught them on the tips of His fingers and flung them out into space and bedecked the heavens with stars. And nobody said a word. The reason nobody said anything, there wasn't anybody there to say anything! So God Himself said, "That's good!"*

Frankly, I want to know the God who long ago moved *"over the surface of the waters"* (Genesis 1:2), Who reached into the void and darkness of pre-creation to bring order out of chaos (He can do that in my life and yours, as well), Who spoke forth light, called the seas into existence, and breathed life into every created thing, man and animal alike (Genesis 1:1ff). This is the God Who hung the moon and the stars on nothing (Job 26:7). I can't even imagine such wonder, power, and splendor.

God defies human reason. The only thing I'm certain about is that He does exist and there is much about Him for which I have no explanation. Albert Camus, a card-carrying atheist and French philosopher, won the Nobel Prize for Literature in 1957. He was killed three years later in a car accident in France.[8] Prior to his death, Camus said, "I would rather live my life as if there is a God and die to find out there isn't, than live as if there isn't (a God) and to die to find out that there is."[9] Me, too. But I am certain of God's existence and that *"he who comes to God must believe that He is* (first things first), *and that He is a rewarder of those who seek Him"* (Hebrews 11:6). Beyond that I have more questions than answers. Except for the theological basics, God remains an enigma.

I vividly recall the day when I got word that, while on a mission trip in Jamaica, a former collegiate player of mine sustained an injury that ended his life. I was blindsided. It was a freak "accident," resulting in the tragic death of a young man full of potential and great promise. He loved the Lord, loved people, and loved serving God. His parents were two wonderful people who had spent their lives in service to God. From a human perspective, his life was cut short. Nobody understood why. I certainly did not, at least, not fully. How could this happen? His death seemed so senseless. I wrote the following to some of his teammates prior to the funeral.

> *I must admit that I don't always like God's decisions. I don't always like what He does and what He chooses not to do. I don't understand. I don't have ready answers to the unexpected, the hurt, the pain, and all the rest; and if I did, they wouldn't be worth much anyway.*
>
> *When it comes to grasping what God is about. I am left with two distinct options: 1) All that has taken place in the last week I trust has deep meaning and fits somehow into God's sovereign scheme (whether I understand it or not); or 2) All that has occurred — the tears, the agony, an empty room where a boy once played, and the grave where a coffin will be laid, has no meaning at all. Take your pick. I choose the former. I believe God knows what He is about.*
>
> *God does not need explaining, nor does He need me to defend His actions. Maybe we shouldn't try. He does what He does without apology and often without full explanation...and that is troublesome for flesh and blood. I have observed that God has never checked in with me (or anyone else for that matter) to first get my (or others') approval on anything He intends to do. He just goes about His divine business — pulling, stretching, poking, pushing, molding, shaping, remaking me (and you) in the process of life's trials — using it all in some strange way (that makes no sense to me) for my ultimate good and for the good of His Kingdom. He does not ask me to understand. He simply asks me to trust Him. There is no real alternative.*

To this day, I still do not get it, but I'm learning to live with the mystery of God and His ways.

In Mitch Alban's New York Times Bestseller book, *Have a Little Faith*, he asked his friend the "Reb," Rabbi Albert Lewis, "How do you know God exists?

The Reb responded, "An excellent question…First, make the case against Him."

Albom suggested that humanity has outgrown belief in God, ever since science has resolved many of the mysteries regarding the universe. God, he thought, is no longer needed or relevant.

"Now," said the Rabbi, "My turn…No matter how small they [scientists] take it back…there is always something they can't explain, something that created it all at the end of the search. And no matter how far they try to go the other way — to extend life, play around with the genes, clone this, clone that, live to one hundred and fifty — at some point, life is over. And then what happens? When life comes to an end? When you come to the end, that's where God begins."[10]

Honestly, I'm thinking that God is too big to miss, and yet we willfully and deliberately manage to do just that every day in every way — suppressing (pushing down) and ignoring the obvious truth about God Himself. The evidence is in. *"His eternal power and divine nature have been clearly seen."* We are without excuse. To ignore the truth is to play the part of a fool (cf. Romans 1:18–22). Tozer's words in his book *The Knowledge of the Holy* are convicting.

> *"If we would bring back spiritual power to our lives, we must begin to think of God more nearly as He is"…(and) the most portentous fact about any man is not what he at a given time may say or do, but what he in his deep heart conceives God to be like."*[11]

I believe in the God of the Bible with all His divine attributes and character (mercy, love, faithfulness, truth, immutability, omniscience, omnipresence, omnipotence, etc.) on display, functioning in this world and throughout history. I believe in the God Who parted the Red Sea and drowned the armies of Egypt, breached the walls of Jericho, enabled a boy with a sling to bring down a giant. I believe in the God Who commands the winds and the waves, opens prison doors, kicks down the gates of Hell, heals the brokenhearted, lifts the head of the downcast, gives strength to the weary, restores the sick, and provides a clear set of life principles and laws, God's very best, designed to *"empower you* [and me] *by its instruction and correction, giving you the strength to take the right direction and lead you deeper into the path of godliness"* (II Timothy 3:16, TPT). I believe that firmly, every bit of it and more, though *"God's grace"* and His actions are clouded in mystery and surprise, and *"made known"* only by divine *"revelation"* (cf. Ephesians 3:1–6, ESV).

In the introduction of Ben Hughes' book, *When God Breaks In*, Lana Vawser described God as:

> *The God who bends down. The God who reaches in. The God who invites. The God who embraces…The God of the suddenly. The God of the unexpected. The God of power. The God of surprise. The God who loves to reveal His nature, His love, His power, and His Word to His people. The God who breaks in and breaks through in our everyday lives…The God of encounter who turns lives around in a moment….The God of hope, the God of healing, the God of deliverance, the God of freedom, the God of provision. Encountering Him will leave you never the same.*[12]

That's the God I must have; the God I must find; the God I must know.

The psalmist declared, *"My soul (my life, my inner self) thirsts for God, for the living God. When will I come and see the face of God?"* (Psalm 42:1–3, AMP). I can answer that. I'll seek God when I'm desperate enough, when I've been backed into a corner and there is no way out, when I've run out of answers, when all hope is gone, when God alone is the only solution. Jesus Himself prayed, *"This is life eternal* [real life] *that they* [a weak, untrustworthy, and disbelieving, hard-pressed bunch] *should know Thee the only true God and Him whom thou didst send, even Jesus Christ"* (John 17:3, KJV).

The Hebrew word to "know" is *yada*. The Greek equivalent is *ginosko*. It means to become acquainted with, to learn with certainty, to discover firsthand, to know by means of personal experience.[13] Knowing God is to hear the Father speak words that challenge and comfort my heart, those wonderful *"words of life,"* recorded in the pages of the Bible. When the Scriptures speak, God speaks directly into my life. To have a genuine knowledge of God is to realize His love for you and me, no matter where we are in life, no matter what we are facing. His love is more than a sign displayed during an NFL game, carried throughout the stadium by an enthusiastic fan (you've all seen him) with wild hair, and captured on national TV — *"John 3:16."* The words are familiar and universal, *"For God so loved the world that He gave His only begotten Son…"* (John 3:16) — a love that is sure and steady and measured at the cross of Christ, a love that will hold you and embrace you every hour of every day until eternity ceases to be. His love is as mysterious and baffling as it gets, but it's real and genuine, and it can be known and experienced. God spoke through the prophet Jeremiah:

> **Jeremiah 9:23–24. NLT** – *This is what the* LORD *says…those who wish to boast should boast in this alone: that they truly know me and understand that I am the* LORD *who demonstrates unfailing love…*

The year 2020 was certainly one of the most trying and disconcerting years on record in my seventy plus trips around the sun. The Covid-19 pandemic destroyed families, isolated friends, and brought fear, financial ruin, and death to many across the world. No one seemed immune to the impact of this deadly virus. After nearly a year of dealing with the turmoil associated with the disease and with no end in sight, a tired, distraught friend asked me a question that many, I'm sure, have voiced, "Is there such a thing as a day without bullcrap?" Is there no end to this? No relief? No escape? I responded:

> *"Not a chance! This is a fallen, broken world we live in. Hardly a day passes without some evidence of that fact. But there is also not a day, not a single moment that goes by, that God is disengaged, disinterested, or uninvolved in my daily life and yours also. He is always working His best for my best, always moving/pushing me in the right direction, His direction, always hearing the deepest cry of my heart and wiping the tears streaming down my face, always intervening in the darkest of days, always using "all things" (the good stuff and the tough stuff) for my good in spite of all the crap I have experienced, seen, and heard (some of which I've created myself). So...yes, lots of "bull" along the way, but also there is lots of grace, strength, and hope for the day to help me carry on till I step through the doors of eternity. "That's my story, and I'm sticking to it."*

*"If the Lord is God, follow Him."* That's where the answer rests. That's where the journey really begins, and that's where it must end — knowing God well enough to go with Him through the ups and downs of daily living and to trust Him with my future. When your thoughts are attuned to God and focused on Him, you will have no trouble deciding to give Him *"first place in everything"* (Colossians 1:18), even in the midst of hardship. You'll sleep better at night.

The South African Andrew Murray (1828–1917) was a gifted speaker, pastor, and author who had a heart for people and a deep love for God and His Word. He enjoyed a highly successful, significant ministry throughout Europe and America, and wrote 240 books (imagine) before his death in 1917 (I've struggled writing three)! His life, however, was not without problems. In 1879, he became ill and lost his voice for two years.[14] He came under criticism in a harsh letter charging him with "teaching error," an unfounded allegation. Twice he had a car accident that left him physically impaired (lame) for the remainder of his life. On another occasion, he fell from a cart and sustained a back injury that hampered him for years. Yet, through it all, Murray remained humble and dependent upon God and the mystery of His sustaining grace. One morning, he penned the following words for his own encouragement:

> *In Time of Trouble Say:*
> *First, He brought me here; it is by His will I*
> *am in this strait place: in that fact I will rest.*
> *Next, He will keep me here in His love, and*
> *give me grace to behave as His child.*
> *Then, He will make the trial a blessing,*
> *teaching me the lessons He intends me to*
> *learn, and working in me the grace He*
> *means to bestow.*
> *Last, in His good time He can bring me out*
> *again — how and when He knows.*
> *Let me say I am here, (1) By God's*
> *appointment, (2) In his keeping, (3) Under*
> *His training, and (4) For His time.*[15]

Your view of God will impact and influence every facet of your life, either positively or negatively. You can count on it, as sure as the sun rises in the east and sets in the west.

Phillip Yancey, in his book *What Good is God?* stated that he came to Bible college with a "distorted image of God" (most of us suffer from the same clouded vision) — an image he claimed took years to undo. He wrote that he saw God:

> *…as a frowning Super-cop looking to squash anyone who might be having a good time. How wrong I was. I have come to know a God who has a soft spot for rebels, who recruits people like the adulterer David, the whiner Jeremiah, the traitor Peter, and the human-rights abuser Saul of Tarsus. I have come to know a God whose Son made prodigals the heroes of his stories and the trophies of his ministry*[16]

Moses knew something about God, but not everything. After forty years of wilderness living, the man was ready to meet God, an experience and encounter that changed the course of his life. That day at the burning bush, when God disrupted Moses' daily routine and called Moses by name (can't get much more personal than that), He revealed Himself to be *"the God of your father, the God of Abraham, Isaac, and Jacob."* The biblical record shows that initially *"Moses* [like the rest of us] *hid his face and was afraid to look at God"* (Exodus 2:6*).* No wonder. God knew of Moses' past, fully aware that he was raised in the lap of luxury and walked the palaces of the rich and famous. He was trained in the best schools Egypt had to offer, steeped in Egyptian culture, and worshipped in the temples of pagan gods. God also knew that Moses murdered a man in his earlier years and then attempted to cover up the crime and bury the evidence. Guilty on all counts. Understandably, the man cowered before the Judge of the universe, fearful of discovery and the consequences his actions might bring.

As he hid his face in shame, Moses discovered the mystery of God, that He has, and continues to have, a "soft spot for rebels," for a murderer, a runaway, and for a smelly, sweaty sheep herder who stuttered and stammered through life. The very fact that God does things differently, sees what we cannot see, and acts in ways we frankly don't understand or approve of, brings hope to the rest of us. We may not appreciate it at first, but He knows what He's doing, and He knows how to get results.

With so little going for him and no credentials to speak of, Moses hears from God. Who would have guessed? Certainly not me. Moses wouldn't have been my first choice given his resume. But the mystery and grace of God took an unworthy man with a shady background and destines him to become the greatest leader Israel has ever known and entrusted him with the task of delivering the good news — that God has not turned a deaf ear to their problems. He had not forgotten them. He knew of their plight. He knew the details of their story. He heard their cries, as He does yours. He was there in the thick of things, in the mud pits of Egypt, and felt the sting of the taskmaster's whip. He would stand with them and show Himself strong on the streets and in the palaces of Egypt to bring the most powerful military of the day to its knees and liberate a nation of slaves bound in chains with no hope and no future. Moses had a decision to make, the most important decision he would ever make, one that would impact eternity — follow God or return to herding sheep in the desert sands of Midian, a nobody going nowhere. It was that simple and no different for me and you. Daily life is a series of choices.

Moses decided he would answer the divine call, somewhat reluctantly at first, but eventually he opts to alter his life goals and change course, as God directed and head out on an adventure he could never have possibly imagined. A man with a checkered past, broken, scared, and unsure of himself and his future, steps up and takes the reigns of leadership as God wanted and leads a people enslaved for four hundred years to freedom. *How* God did this sort of thing remains a mystery. *Why* God does this sort of thing is another story. He rescues, delivers, and liberates to show forth His amazing, wonderful grace, to demonstrate His unfathomable mercy, to embrace a flawed, unfit man and an undeserving people with unconditional love, to keep His word and fulfill His promise, and He did it and does it all for the glory of His name — *"so that all the peoples of the earth may know that the LORD is God and that there is no other"* (I Kings 8:60, NIV). The ways of God remain a mystery.

The people of Israel watched in awe as this great God took up their cause and destroyed the heart and will of a mighty king, and then led them on the journey of a lifetime. At first, it was a cloud by day to guide them and a pillar of fire at night to shield them from harm. Later, it was the Ark of the Covenant and the Tabernacle, the place of meeting where God and man would come together.

When Israel arrived on the banks of the Red Sea, fearful and anxious for their future, with seemingly no means of escape, the sea at their backs, mountains to the right and left, and hundreds of Pharaoh's finest chariots closing in for the kill, the people were told to *"Stand by* [Shut up! Quit your whining and complaining — my paraphrase.] *and see the salvation of the Lord which He will accomplish for you today"* (Exodus 14:13). Words to live or die by. No one could have predicted what was to come. Their journey brought them to a crossroad, the same place we all get to eventually. Follow God, or come up with your own ideas and take your chances. Seek the face of God and the security and mystery of His presence and power or go toe-to-toe battling the sword and wrath of Pharaoh. Either stand with God or stand alone in the world. Make up your mind.

It didn't (and doesn't) seem like much of a choice. There was really no one and nowhere else to go to secure their well-being and their future. But isn't that how God operates, deliberately leading us into a place of faith where eventually we have to depend on Him, and leave things in His capable hands to fix what's gone wrong in our lives? Seek God and His advice or ignore Him and reap the consequences of a poor decision. Moses and the people made an extremely wise choice given their circumstance. We might consider their reliance upon God at that moment as a model for our own lives.

I'm sure that by the end of day the Israelites were glad they knew God, that they had opted to follow His lead, kept their mouths shut, and let God enter the battle on their behalf. I'm even more sure that they were happier that God knew them. *"The God of Abraham, Isaac, and Jacob,"* revealed Himself once again to be the great "I Am" — the God who makes things happen (and He certainly did that) — a lesson about God we would all do well to learn and remember.

He fed them, clothed them, protected them, and freed a nation of slaves — a firsthand experience with the Lord who brought Egypt to her knees. The plagues, the terrible Angel of Death dispatched by God to sweep across Egypt, the opening of the Red Sea, the total annihilation of the pursuing Egyptian army, all of it used by God to help men and women better grasp Who He is and deepen their understanding of their *"knowledge of the Lord, (that) He is God; (and) there is no other besides Him"* (Deuteronomy 4:35). That's the God we would be wise to follow. A really smart move.

Henry T. Blackaby, who wrote, *Experiencing the Spirit: The Power of Pentecost Every Day,* pointed out that Christianity is not simply believing the truths of the Bible. Rather, it's acting on them and allowing God to control our daily lives. "You must respond," Blackaby wrote, "to God and make the choice to interact personally with Him."[17] He is no longer a "mystery." Don't miss the obvious. He is not hiding. He is not the "flea" without legs you may have misjudged. Make the decision. Follow God in Christ…without reservation or hesitation, and you unlock God's best for your life.

> *"Jesus became what we are, that He might makes us what He is."*[1]
> —Athanasius of Alexandria (293–373 AD),
> Christian theologian and Church Father

# 6

# THE GOD WHO PUT ON SKIN

When the *"angel of the Lord"* showed up in Joseph's dreams to set his thinking straight (and we all can use a little of that), the man had been struggling with Mary's unexpected pregnancy, and rightly so. "What has Mary done? Who has she been with? What do I do now with this mess?" Joseph was clearly *"turning the matter over in his mind"* (Matthew 1:20, PHILLIPS), desperately looking for answers.

The gospel of Matthew records the angel's message sent by God to a bewildered Joseph. *"Do not be afraid to take Mary as your wife"* (Matthew 1:20, NLT) — a clear challenge to step into God's plans. He knows what He's doing, how it is to be done, and what He wants to accomplish in the life of this man and his future bride — a life principle we would do well to remember when the pressure is on. The angel confirmed that Mary, Joseph's wife to be, had not cheated on him, though she was with child. She was destined by divine intervention (the supernatural work of the Holy Spirit) to *"bear a Son,"* Who would play the role of Savior/Deliverer/Redeemer/Priest/King, and *"save his people from their sins"* (Matthew 1:20–21). The world would come to know him as Jesus, *"God is salvation"* — a child with an uncommon future, born into a common household, and given a common name. He had but one title in those early days — *"Immanuel, which translated means, 'God with us'"* (Matthew 1:23), an unmistakable, definitive identity. *"God became one of us"* (TPT) to live out His days with a single-minded goal, to set at liberty those imprisoned by their own moral failure and weaknesses (cf. Luke 4:18–19) and to provide each man and woman the opportunity to leave yesterday behind, wipe the slate clean, and start anew. It doesn't get any better than that for me. *"The past is finished and gone, everything has become fresh and new"* (II Corinthians 5:17, PHILLIPS). A remarkable revelation, the plan and Person of God showing up in my neighborhood to help the likes of me (an undeserving, stubborn rebel) live an extraordinary, meaningful, fully satisfying life, which includes peace with God, a new direction and purpose for getting up each morning, the hope of Heaven and eternity in the future, and most importantly, living each day in a personal, loving relationship with God. This is the God Who laid His royal robes aside, left Heaven with nothing in hand, and came to this world that you and I might have everything we need to live fully and successfully — the sovereign God of the universe, Who spoke all things into existence, Who deliberately replaced the grandeur and comfort of His palace for a back-alleyway manger and a bed of straw, and *"no place to lay His head"* (Luke 9:58, AMP). It's unimaginable, unheard of among gods of lesser caliber.

Theologians refer to this as the Incarnation when God put on skin — the greatest, most profound, theological truth of all, God purposefully leaving His heavenly throne to live and die as a man in a chaotic, despairing environment, willingly and gladly stepping out of eternity to enter our finite world with but one holy objective, *"to seek and to save"* (Luke 19:10, NIV) you and me (and we certainly need a lot of that) — the eternal King sacrificing Himself for the welfare of His subjects. The incarnation is a story of grace — God making Himself known, when He didn't have to do it. He could have remained hidden, and nobody would have been the wiser. He could have stayed right where He was — unconcerned, uninvolved, angry and vindictive, watching the world go to hell in a handbasket. It is, after all, what we deserve. But He doesn't. He does a surprising thing, which catches all humanity off guard. He shows up on our streets, as the Lover of your soul and mine — a remarkable love story about a God worth finding, knowing, and following.

Max Lucado described God's arrival this way:

> *His first home was a palace. Servants were at his fingertips. The snap of his fingers changed the course of history. His name was known and loved. He had everything — wealth, power, respect. And then he had nothing…How could a king lose everything in one instant? One moment he was royalty; the next he was in poverty… He knew what it was like to be rained on, to be cold. He knew what it was like to have no home. In His kingdom he had been revered; now he was ridiculed. His neighbors tried to lynch him. Some called him a lunatic. His family tried to confine him to their house. Those who didn't ridicule him tried to use him. They wanted favors. They wanted tricks… He was accused of a crime he had never committed. Witnesses were hired to lie. The jury was rigged. No lawyer was assigned to his defense. A judge swayed by politics handed down the death penalty. They killed him. He left as he came — penniless. He was buried in a borrowed grave, his funeral financed by compassionate friends. Though he once had everything, he died with nothing.*[2]

Every doctrine of historic Christianity recorded in and gleaned from the pages of Scripture is contingent upon that one, single fact — the coming of God into the world. He *"became flesh"* (John 1:14) and *"let Himself out for us to see"* (John 1:18). The New American Standard Bible translates that phrase as *"He (Jesus, the Word made flesh) has explained Him (God)."* The verb *"explain"* (*exegeomai*) means "to introduce Himself" or "to reveal Himself." God explaining God. It cannot be otherwise. Only infinity and the omniscience of God (and the other attributes of God) can define, for instance, *"the end from the beginning, and from ancient times the things that are not yet done"* (Isaiah 46:10, NIV).

Buzz Lightyear of *Toy Story* fame (Pixar, Walt Disney,1995) believed that he could do the impossible and go *"to infinity and beyond."* Not happening in the world of men. No man can grasp the concept *"from everlasting to everlasting"* (Psalm 90:2, ESV). The boundlessness of eternity and the God Who lives there and here simultaneously escapes us. We have no clue, not really…not unless one day God opts to engage us and reveal His true self, and He has done just that in Christ. Mercifully, He continuously shows Himself to a spiritually ignorant, thankless world that otherwise would not know Him or recognize Him, except of course He smacks us behind the head to awake our dull senses. I have felt that "wake-up call" a few times in my life.

The true personality of God is revealed in the person of Jesus — the tears He shed outside the tomb of Lazarus, His compassion for a woman who messed up her life and was caught in adultery, His concern for a rich man with misplaced values, and His righteous anger directed at the hypocrisy of the Pharisees, all this and more — the perfect expression of God Himself, coming down to the one and only place in the known universe that can sustain life. It is where we live out our mortal lives, planet Earth — on the "Pale Blue Dot" (the name given to a picture taken from space by Voyager 1, 1977) of which Carl Sagan, the Pulitzer Prize-winning astronomer, rightly observed…

> *Look again at that dot. That's here. That's home. That's us. On it everyone you love, everyone you know, everyone you ever heard of, every human being who ever was, lived out their lives. The aggregate of our joy and suffering, thousands of confident religions, ideologies, and economic doctrines, every hunter and forager, every hero and coward, every creator and destroyer of civilization, every king and peasant, every young couple in love, every mother and father, hopeful child, inventor and explorer, every teacher of morals, every corrupt politician, every "superstar," every "supreme leader," every saint and sinner in the history of*

> our species lived there — on a mote of dust suspended in a sunbeam.
>
> *The Earth is a very small stage in a vast cosmic arena. Think of the rivers of blood spilled by all those generals and emperors so that, in glory and triumph, they could become the momentary masters of a fraction of a dot. Think of the endless cruelties visited by the inhabitants of one corner of this pixel on the scarcely distinguishable inhabitants of some other corner, how frequent their misunderstandings, how eager they are to kill one another, how fervent their hatreds. Our posturing, our imagined self-importance, the delusion that we have some privileged position in the universe, are challenged by this point of pale light. Our planet is a lonely speck in the great enveloping cosmic dark. In our obscurity, in all this vastness, there is no hint that help will come from elsewhere to save us from ourselves.[3]*

And yet, help did arrive. God put on flesh, and when He did, the face of God became evident in the face of Jesus. The miracle is that God would consider coming at all to "a mote of dust," an inconsequential, insignificant, obscure planet located in the vast darkness of space, a place ruined by its rebellious inhabitants whose moral behavior was/is less than stellar. For reasons known only to God, He decided to show up at our front door to invite us to an extraordinary adventure and to follow Him faithfully through the years. He came to "save us from ourselves" and redeem the whole lot of us.

Apparently, we are not as insignificant as some may have once thought, at least not in the eyes of God, for He has found damaged people worth rescuing and redeeming. "Amazing grace, how sweet the sound." The Apostle Paul, who referred to himself (cf. I Timothy 1:15) as the worst of all sinners (I could compete with Him for that title) wrote, *"God (Himself rescued us from dead-end alleys and dark dungeons. He's set us up in the kingdom of the Son He loves so much, the Son who got us out of the pit we were in, got rid of the sins we were doomed to keep repeating"* (Colossians 1:13–14, MSG).

A former student of mine admitted that as a young child her experience with God was virtually "nonexistent." Her daily life had become harsh and brutal. Her parents sent her out to beg for money until she was no longer useful to them. And when she broke her leg at ten years old, she was callously abandoned and forced to fend for herself on the streets. Eventually, she was placed in an orphanage for "crippled, handicapped and disabled children" — a lost, fearful, brokenhearted little girl discarded by those who were supposed to love her and a society that viewed her as useless and cursed. Such despair and hopelessness. She wrote, "I didn't know anything about God..."

But that would soon change. God put on skin and showed up at the door of the orphanage in the person of an American Christian couple who took her in, adopted her, embraced her, loved her with the love of Christ, and taught her about the God who rescues and saves, the God who invited her (and the rest of us) with open, loving arms — *"Come to Me all who are weary and heavy laden, and I will give you rest. Take My yoke upon you and learn from Me, for I am gentle and humble in heart, and you will find rest for your souls. For My yoke is easy and My burden is light"* (Matthew 11:28030, NIV). She said, "I wanted to know who this God was, what made him so different than the Buddha I worshiped." She found out — the day the incarnate God walked into the orphanage and touched her life.

What God goes out of His way to do such things and moves in mercy and power to alter the life of a little girl (and anyone else for that matter) for the better? Jesus of Nazareth, the son of a carpenter, the *"image of the invisible God"* (Colossians 1:15), Who loves us and *"gave Himself up for"* us (Ephesians 5:25), that's Who! He is *"the full explanation of who God truly is"* (John 1:18, TPT) — the God who values His creation and finds worth in a ten-year-old orphan that nobody cared about or wanted, and sees merit and significance in the rest of us, a sorry, obstinate, independent-minded group of self-serving individuals, of whom I am one. In coming to our world, God showed

Himself to be kindhearted, longsuffering, merciful, caring, holy, moral, forgiving, supportive, involved, sacrificial, and effective (etc.) in carrying out His redemptive plans to benefit His less-than-perfect creatures (that's humankind). He chose of His own will to intersect our lives as the Good Shepherd, seeking out lost sheep, the Father who waits patiently for the prodigal son to come home, the Defender of the downtrodden who *"rides the heavens to our help"* (Deuteronomy 33:26), and the *"King of kings and the Lord of lords"* (Revelation 19:16) who someday will return with sword unsheathed to make all things right. David wrote confidently of God that He is:

> **Psalm 18:2, TPT** – *"… as real to me as bedrock beneath my feet like a castle on a cliff, my forever firm fortress, my mountain of hiding, my pathway of escape, my tower of rescue where none can reach me. My secret strength and shield around me, you are salvation's ray of brightness shining on the hillside, always the champion of my cause."*

Frankly, I would be less than a fool not to follow this God, or obey His commands, or trust His good judgment in directing my daily affairs. He is after all, *"always the champion of my cause."* That was, is, and continues to be His focus and intent from eternity past — to bring a comprehensive, all-expense-paid plan and purpose to my life, designed by His love and wisdom for my benefit and His glory.

For the first time in history, more than two thousand years ago, *"the Word"* (Jesus), Who always was God (cf. John 1:1), entered the world *"in the likeness of men"* (cf. Philippians 2:6–7), and did so as a baby lying in a dirty old stable — the most surprising, unimpressive place for a King to be born. A few shepherds and some wise men followed a star that brought them to a stable in the back streets of Bethlehem. There they got an up-close-and-personal glimpse of *"the eternal God"* (Romans 16:26), *"the Lord Most High"* (Psalm 7:17), Who later walked the highways and byways of the ancient world and lived as an ordinary man, a blue-collar worker, employed in the family business. Like most of us, He had neighbors, brothers and sisters, and a mother and father who had trouble keeping tabs on Him (cf. Mark 6:3). Most days, He hung out with His fishing buddies (cf. Luke 5:1–11), just regular guys trying to scratch out a living. On one occasion, He changed the heart of a *"town harlot"* (cf. Luke 7:36–50, MSG) who wept with remorse and regret over the life she had lived. He visited a home in Cana to celebrate the wedding of a family friend (cf. John 2:1–11). On another day, He stopped long enough to put mud on the eyes of a blind man to give him sight for the first time in his life — *"that the works of God might be displayed in him"* (John 9:3). He showed up in the city of Nain just in time to stop a coffin on the way to the cemetery, so He might purposely reach out and touch the face of death and give life back to the only son of a widow (cf. Luke 7:11–16). Many in the crowd that day, who witnessed this remarkable display of power and mercy agreed — *"God has visited His people today"* (Luke 7:16, NLT). Indeed He had. Later, as He passed through Jericho, Jesus stopped to have lunch with a tax collector, a man despised by others (cf. Luke 19:1–10) but loved and accepted by God, the God who actively and deliberately seeks to reveal Himself as the great Lover of my soul.

What God does such things? The disciples wanted to know. I want to know. They had reservations, questions, concerns, and so they asked to see the Father. The answer was standing before their very eyes all along. St. Athanasius the Great, the Father of Orthodoxy, observed (approximately 323 AD), "Even on the cross He (God) did not hide Himself from sight; rather, He made all creation witness to the presence of its Maker."[4]

Jesus explained to His troubled followers, *"I've been with you all this time and you still don't know who I am? How could you ask me to show you the Father, for anyone who has looked at me has seen the Father"* (John 14:9, TPT). If you see Jesus, you see God. If you know Jesus, you know God. If you walk with Jesus, you walk with God. In no uncertain terms, He announced, *"I and the Father are one"* (John 10:30). Lean back and rest your head on the chest of Christ, and like John of old (cf. John 13:23), you will hear the heartbeat of God. Look into His eyes (like the writer to the Hebrews may have done), and you will see the very *"radiance of His (God's) glory and the exact representation of His nature"* (Hebrews 1:3). He is, wrote John, *"the Light that bursts through the gloom"* (John 1:5, TPT).

I don't know about you. Sometimes I could use a little "Light" to break through the darkness and misery of my day. The Incarnation is that light, assuring me that God is here, and that He has come to make Himself known and mercifully impact my life with His goodness. He has never loved me (and you, too) from a distance. He has never loved me more than He does today. In fact, He has always loved me in the now, right where I am, in the craziness of daily living, in my failures (and I've had plenty of those), in my successes (few they may be), and when I've feared the most, scared to death of what tomorrow may bring. Yet, God journeys with me through thick and thin. *"I will be with you; I will not fail you or forsake you"* (Joshua 1:5) is His unwavering promise. Simply, His love and care for me sticks like that *"one loving friend,"* Solomon mentions *"who is joined to your heart"* (Proverbs 18:14, TPT), whose intentions and motives are pure. He left Heaven, bending low to *"[pick up] the poor from out of the dirt, [and] rescue the wretched who've been thrown out with the trash"* (Psalm 113:5–7, MSG). That's the God I must discover, get to know, seek, follow, and serve, the only God who took the time to search me out, rummaging around in the rubble of my foolish behavior and moral deficiencies, showing up in His skin to grab me and radically transform my life for the better. No other god in any religion is interested in pursuing me or helping me to that extent — only the Incarnate God of the Bible, Jesus. I owe Him my life.

From the very start of the human epoch, God came looking for Adam and Eve in the Garden of Eden to redeem their botched lives. Likewise, God approached Noah with the blueprints for building the Ark, designed to rescue and ensure the man's safety and that of his family. God initiated contact with Abraham and sent him off down an unknown path with a promise to bless his journey. Where would Abraham be had he (or any of us) decided not to follow God's leading? God found Moses in the lonely, hot, dry sands of the Midian desert and changed the course of his life. God interrupted Joshua's plans the night before the battle for the city of Jericho to tell him that the *"Captain of the host of the Lord"* (Joshua 5:14) had arrived to takeover. Good news. When God puts on skin and draws near, there is no need to tremble at life any longer. No need to be dismayed, worried, or fearful of the height and depth of the "walls" you are facing — *"the Lord your God is with you wherever you go"* (Joshua 1:9), be it in the unemployment line, the hospital, the funeral home, or the divorce courts. Those walls will come down because the God who puts on skin has already shown up for you and for so many others down through the centuries.

It was Jesus who invaded the lives of fishermen by the lake of Gennesaret and called them by name to do something more with their lives than they were currently doing. God stopped Saul of Tarsus on the road to Damascus with a new plan for his life. It's always the same…God reaching to man, to me, to you… never the other way around.

I have seen God in the hospital wards bringing much needed healing of body and soul to the hopeless and the sick. I have known God to show up in mercy and power at the bars and crack houses to break the chains of self-destructive addiction in the lives of men and women who have no purpose beyond the next fix. I've watched God at Walmart (yes, Walmart) stocking shelves and stopping long enough to help an elderly woman load her car with groceries. I've known God to show up in the soup kitchens feeding and clothing the poor and the desolate. I have seen Him running to the homes of wrecked marriages where two broken people, who once loved each other, are now weeping in desperate need of restoration, relational healing, and emotional and spiritual health. I have heard God comfort mourners, speaking gentle words of encouragement and reassurance, wiping away tears, and strengthening pallbearers carrying the coffin of their father and friend. I've have seen God reach out His strong, reassuring arms to meet the practical needs of a widow and ease her fearful, anxious heart. *"When you pass through the deep, stormy sea, you can count on Me to be there with you"* (Isaiah 43:2 (TPT). That's the God I want to know, the

God I want to follow, the God I want to trust, the God I want to love *"because He first loved (me)"* (I John 4:19), the God with skin who personally reaches into my world and draws me close.

On August 5, 2010, a one-hundred-year-old San José mine in Chili collapsed, trapping thirty-three men more than 2,000 feet below unstable dirt and rock. They had no provisions to speak of, just some cans of tuna fish, a few packages of cookies, and "a mere ten bottles of water," and little hope of getting out alive. There was no escape. They were alone in a situation that few survive. The news media set their chances for survival at a mere two percent The odds were stacked against them. For sixty-nine days they struggled, suffered, and feared the worst. Reuters reported that Franklin Lobos, a former professional soccer player, who was among the victims, later said, "This was the toughest match of my life."[5] No doubt it was. The battle was to stay alive against overwhelming odds. In moments like that, you had better know of God's unlimited love and power to rescue and save, and His uncanny ability and desire to bring good out of tragedy. And He did just that, through the efforts of a team of rescue workers who simply would not give up. They found a way, when there seemed to be no way (sounds like God to me) and bored a hole in the ground the size of a grapefruit to pass down much needed supplies, letters from family members, and a Bible, the book describing the character and person of God. And hope was born. The uncle of the first man to emerge from the darkness of a would-be grave put things in perspective. He simply said, "This is a miracle from God."[6] Of course it was. *"Nothing, you see, is impossible with God"* (Luke 1:38, MSG). Only He could have pulled this off. The witnesses admitted that God was involved from start to finish. He had mercifully intervened. He was there, buried beneath the rubble with the miners. And it was a good thing, too, for God knows how to bust out of a tomb covered over with stone and walk out to face a new day. He's done it before. One miner who stepped out of the rescue cage was heard to say, "I am so happy…I have been with God."[7] And so he was. In the darkest place the man had ever been, he and thirty-two others held the hand of God, and the whole world marveled and heard it, saw it…a testimony to the presence, goodness, and mercy of the God who put on skin. The most important decision those men ever made was to entrust their lives to Him, the God who came and entered their world, deep within the pit of a collapsed mine, and He's been doing it for us all ever since time began — the God who put on skin.

*"Never let the truth get in the way of a good story."*
—Mark Twain

# 7

# THE REALITY OF GOD: THE TRUTH AND NOTHING BUT THE TRUTH

Sharlene Landau was outside pruning her roses when she heard a loud thump and a cry. She immediately dropped her tools and ran to her four-year-old son, Alex. She found him lying at the bottom of the stairs in the garage. Apparently, he had jumped from the top, trying to fly like Peter Pan. After a long talk about reality versus make believe, Sharlene walked away feeling fairly confident that she had gotten her point across…until she heard her son whisper, "Must not have been enough pixie dust!"[1]

The search for God has only two options: reality or make believe. There is a huge difference between the two. On one hand, if you search and find God, you find life and a vibrant, effective faith that works day in and day out, no matter where you are and what you are up against. By faith, Noah built himself a boat. Sarah got pregnant at an old age. Rahab survived Israel's attack on Jericho. *"Faith,"* said the writer to the Hebrews, *"imparted power to make them* [followers of God facing persecution] *strong"*(Hebrews11:34, PTP). In sharp contrast, search worldwide for make-believe gods of lesser substance (imitations of the real thing) and your efforts will end in disappointment, discontent, and delusion. *"The path of the righteous,"* sang Isaiah, *"is smooth and level"* (Isaiah 26:7, TPT). In either case, pixie dust does not work well. What does work is this: "Before a man can see God, God must first have sought the man...We pursue God because, and only because, He has first put an urge with us that spurs us to the pursuit."[2] The search for the reality of God begins and ends with God.

Ethan the Ezrahite thoughtfully looked back over the years (a good practice to follow) and wrote a song about what he had experienced and seen throughout his lifetime — the unmistakable, irrefutable evidence of God's presence and His faithfulness, mercy and power at work in his own life and in the lives of people. *"I will sing of the lovingkindness of the Lord forever* (Psalm 89:1), probably rose to the top of Israel's song charts between 609–598 BC! For Ethan, knowing God was like *"walking on air"* (Psalm 89:17, MSG) — exciting, exhilarating, and terrifying all at the same time. I've had similar experiences. The realization and truth that God exists, and was/is active and personally involved in his daily life (as in yours and mine) brought hope, comfort, and a new enthusiasm for living in this world. It always does, especially when you discover (v. 17, MSG) God's *"well-muscled arm and grip of steel"* (I love that description), and then watch Him "flex" those divine muscles to ensure that His plans for your life will be fully accomplished. *"Nobody,"* observed Ethan, *"messes with [God]"* (Psalm 89:18, MSG). The reality of God is no fantasy. It is the truth. He is for real. That is what Ethan sang about.

In 1944, the world was at war, nation set against nation. Death and destruction were everywhere. Evil was on the march. If ever there was a time and need for knowing God, it was then. Ruth Caye Jones, a housewife, sat down and penned these words, later set to music and sung by George Beverly Shea for the Billy Graham Crusades.[3]

---

*In times like these you need a Savior,*
*In times like these you need an anchor;*

# The Most Important Decision You'll Ever Make

*Be very sure, be very sure*
*Your anchor holds and grips the Solid Rock!*
*This Rock is Jesus, Yes, He's the One;*
*This Rock is Jesus, the only One!*
*Be very sure, be very sure*
*Your anchor holds and grips the Solid Rock!*

---

Ethan drew but one conclusion, the only one possible, after surveying the events and circumstances of his personal life. *"You will find nothing or no one quite like God"* (Psalm 89:6, MSG). *"Who is like (God)?"* he asked. The answer is rock solid and certain — He was, He is, and He forever shall be the Anchor for my soul. You can count on Him through thick and thin, in abundance and in poverty, in sickness and in health. The reality of God makes the difference every single day, be it a good day or one filled with turbulence. The most important decision you will ever make is to seek Him. Find Him. Follow Him. Serve Him, and you will *"walk on air,"* too. That's as real as it gets.

A former colleague of mine reflected on his recent battle with Covid-19, which nearly cost him his life. He wrote passionately of how God pulled him through the horrors of that awful disease. He gained insight and perspective while lying in a hospital bed amidst "the moans and the screams of pain from people trying to just breathe." In the end, he admonished his friends to "reach out and get to know God. God is there and He desires a relationship with (you), and we need to desire it even more (than we have in the past)." Good advice learned in the sometimes cruel realities of a near-death experience. "We are to come into His presence boldly and in confidence," wrote R.C. Sproul. "There is no need to retreat from Him, or to hesitate to enter. But when we come we must remember two things; who He is and who we are."[4]

Having lived and viewed life through the lens of the horrors of a Nazi concentration camp, Corrie ten Boom learned the importance of knowing God intimately, apart from which she never would have survived. Here is what she learned:

> *If you look at the world, you'll be distressed.*
> *If you look within, you'll be depressed.*
> *But if you look at Christ, you'll be at rest.*[5]

Born in the pits of a living hell, her strong words about the reality of a strong God are reassuring for the rest of us. She knew where to look…to Christ. Her faith stood the test. Her spirit remained remarkably resilient throughout that awful ordeal and beyond, and her life became a living tribute and testimony to the reality of God. She learned to *"walk on air,"* to live each day in light of the truth about God.

The Scottish priest, Walter Mill, was charged with heresy and later burned at the stake (1558) for his reformation beliefs and the truth of the gospel to which he was fully committed. When asked to recant his beliefs, he answered:

> *I would rather forfeit ten thousand lives than give up a particle of the heavenly principles…So this day I praise God that He has called me to be among those servants, and seal up the truth with my life, which I received from Him and willingly offer it back to Him for His glory.*

Mills lost his life, but the flames lit that day would light the way for the Reformation of Scotland two years later (1560). That was his mission — not for feeble or lesser men, but for one man who knew the reality of God at the deepest of levels and changed a nation to give birth to the Scottish Presbyterian Church.[6] He *"walked on air"* with every step to the stake.

I have to ask myself, "How different would my life be if I truly knew and trusted the God of the Bible in the deepest parts of my soul?" Would I respond more surely, without panic when life seems to be falling apart? Spurgeon said, "I have a great need for Christ. I have a great Christ for my need."[7] A powerful reality.

Would I be happier, settled, more appreciative of every day, and approach life with a greater sense of hope and peace in my heart? Would I recognize that God will be God and not get so upset about the mundane, ordinary, sometimes annoying little affairs that don't seem to work out as I would like? Would I be able to better handle the tragic, unexpected events that so often take place in my little corner of the world? Philip Yancy asked himself this:

> *How life would differ if I truly played to an audience of One, if I continually asked not "What do I want to do?"...but "What would God have me do?" Certainly my sense of ego and rivalry would fade because I would no longer need to worry about proving myself to other people. I could concentrate instead on pleasing God, by living in such a way that would attract people to Jesus' style of life. My standard of success would also change...nothing is more important than loving God and loving our neighbors.*[8]

How I view God, how deeply I am able to know Him, hear Him speak into my life, and see His heart at work is vital to living each day in confidence, fully trusting Him with every detail. When I calculate God into the equation, I am divinely equipped to better handle everyday stress and strain, and come to terms with personal loss, unwelcomed pain and suffering, unexpected disappointments and setbacks, a multitude of failures, and the frequent madness associated with my daily experiences, and most importantly, to make life count while the opportunity is still available.

Mickey Mantle, one of pro baseball's greatest homerun hitters (I remember watching and idolizing him as a young boy), stood before the national sports press (July 1995). Mantle had a distinguished career with the New York Yankees, a fourteen-time MLB All-Star. He was, however, an alcoholic for most of his adult life, which had taken its toll on his body. His face drawn and his body frail and feeble, he was but a shadow of the man he once was.

During the press conference, Mantle commented on his life. "God gave me a great body and an ability to play baseball," he said. "God gave me everything, and I just…pffft" — a painful admission and reminder that he had blown it — lost opportunities, lost years. "Don't be like me," was his advice.[9]

A reporter asked Mantle if he had signed a donor card. He responded, "Everything I've got is worn out. Although I've heard people say they'd like to have my heart…it's never been used"[10] — an honest, truthful assessment of a life lived apart from the reality of God and God's word, which is *"perfect, reviving the soul [and] making wise the simple"* (Psalm 19:7, ESV). The beat of his "heart" was far from God and, at sixty-three years old, he breathed his last, finishing his journey with regret and sorrow. He had never known a life lived in the knowledge of God who wanted nothing less than the best for him, a reality Mantle simply missed. Except for a few moments of fleeting glory, when he swung for fence and made sports history, he squandered most of his personal life. A tragic story.

Shortly after her husband's death, "when the rains have fallen, and cold winds have blown, and dark clouds have swept across the sky," Susannah Spurgeon, wife of Charles, wrote the following:

> *The soul that has learned the blessed secret of seeing God's hand in all that concerns it cannot be a prey to fear, it looks beyond all second causes, straight into the heart and will of God, and rests content, because He rules.*

It is mercy that our lives are not left for us to plan, but that our Father chooses for us; else might we sometimes turn away from our best blessings, and put from us the choicest, loveliest gifts of His providence.

> *Lord, You have told me who You are, You have in mercy revealed Yourself to me, I know You to be that blessed "gift of God" which alone can save and satisfy my soul. The depth and*

> *compass of heavenly love are manifested in You, and You have shown me, not my need only, but the sufficiency of Your grace and power to meet it. I am an empty sinner; You are a full Christ!*[11]

She knew the truth, the reality of God.

The demands of life in a fractured, broken world are easier met when a truer picture of God is acquired, when I see "the blessed secret of God's hand." It is the difference between joy and haplessness, hope and despair, function and disfunction — the difference between living life on an emotional rollercoaster or being *"still"* and living in peace, security, and stability because you know God (cf. Psalm 46:10). It is the difference between enjoying an intimate relationship with the God of the universe you have come to trust and know or just getting by, floundering through the day with no real purpose or genuine connection to Him. The reality of experiencing God remains the difference between being a citizen of His kingdom wanting to bring heaven down to earth and see God's rule and life principles implemented here and now, or being a citizen of this world living under the tyranny of the moment and whatever philosophical ideal, popular social movement, or cultural norm currently in place. It is the difference between real life and the slow but sure death of the soul. Jesus gave us a strong clue as to what we need to know.

> **John 14:6–7, TPT** – *"I am the Way, I am the Truth, and I am the Life. No one comes next to the Father except through union with me. To know me is to know my Father too. And from now on you will realize that you have seen him and experienced him."*

Words of incredible power and clarity — a summary declaration of God's Person and His eternal plan. The revelation of God is certainly mind-boggling, but it gives me perspective and insight and a better understanding of who I am, where I am, and how I am to negotiate daily routines. Get that right and everyday falls into place, especially when life marches you into the "arena" to be devoured by the harsh realities of living (and dying) in an unpredictable, punishing world (cf. Hebrews 11:36–38). How you see God directly impacts how you walk through the day and the long nights, how you feel, and what you do. We need to know God better than we do. Mark Batterson rightly concluded:

> *All our identity issues are fundamental misunderstandings of who God is. Guilt issues are fundamental misunderstanding of God's grace. Control issues are a misunderstanding of God's sovereignty. Anger issues are a misunderstanding of God's mercy. Pride issues are a misunderstanding of God's greatness. Trust issues are a misunderstanding of God's goodness. If you struggle with any of those issues, it's time to let God be the loudest voice in your life.*[12]

Following "the most extensive and sensitive" three-year study of religion ever conducted (1700 respondents answered 400 questions on American religion and spirituality), sociologists at Baylor's Institute for Studies of Religion concluded: "If I know your image of God, I can tell all kinds of things about you. It's a central part of worldview, and it's linked to how you think about the world in general."[13]

Andy Richter, the former co-host of Late Night With Conan O'Brien was asked by the media (*The Onion*), "Is there a God?" He replied:

> *I don't think so. I don't know. I don't think about it much, because I figure, what's the point? I don't know if it's agnosticism. There are things that are beyond our comprehension, so why bother?...When you pray, I don't think anyone's listening...I don't think anyone cares...I don't think there's anybody sitting in the sky watching you. You're on your own.*[14]

Now, that's a worldview I'm not too excited about. Pointless. Hopeless. Nonsense.

Certainly not a *"walking on air"* philosophy of life.

The answer, "I don't know" may be fine for some, but for those who want the "truth and nothing but the truth" about God, it is hardly adequate. Once your feet hit the grave and you are being lowered into a six-foot hole, the search for God is over. The truth will be revealed, and you will see God whether you want to or not.

Chuck Palahniuk, who wrote *Fight Club* and four other novels, had a somewhat different perspective when asked the same question, "Is there a God?"

"Yes," he responded.

"Care to elaborate?" the interviewer inquired.

"Boy. Let me get back to you when I'm dead."[15]

A bit humorous? Yes. But the most important question of all regarding the existence and identity of God was left unanswered. Unsure and uncomfortable, he played it off as folly since he wasn't sure what he believed. He remained unconvinced and skeptical.

I had a student one time write in a class assignment, "I think that everyone's beliefs are right. [Seriously?] It doesn't matter what you believe, just that you believe in something. I wouldn't want to offend anyone by challenging their beliefs." If I believe that Sponge Bob Square Pants holds the answer to the great issues of life, death, and eternity, I deserve to be challenged and should be.

For Elisabeth Elliot, who served God in the Amazon jungle, the central question about life was not, "'How does this make me feel?' but simply, 'Is this true?' If so, then the next question was, 'What do I need to do about it to obey God?'"[16] Apparently, the truth is crucial to how one lives. The truth informs one's faith, defines one's behavior, and demands an appropriate response in keeping with reality. You cannot make sound, critical, informed decisions apart from the truth.

Now, the young man in question is certainly free to hold to his system of thought and defend it vigorously, and I encouraged him to do so. However, it does matter what one believes. Life teaches us that.

Not all beliefs are equally true, and they all cannot possibly be right. Contradictions exist. I recall a plaque I found some years ago in a gift shop. It simply read, "The truth remains the truth even if no one believes it. A lie is still a lie, even if everyone believes it." Insightful and accurate. Truth must correspond to reality — the way things are, or run the risk of unanticipated, disastrous consequences.

What if you calculated the distance and speed of an approaching train and were thoroughly convinced in your mind that you could beat the train across the tracks before the railroad safety bar went down? If you were in a hurry, you might take a run at it. We do what we believe and believe in what we do. But what if you unknowingly miscalculated, got the numbers mixed up, or failed to consider acceleration factors, distance, time, angle of approach, etc., but you made the attempt anyway, *sincerely* believing with all your heart and mind that you were right and could pull this off? Would it matter what you believe? Of course, it would. Failure to get the facts straight and act appropriately in response to the truth would make you a very sincere but dead man. That's reality. It's not just about *what* you believe that's important, but *why* you believe. Why this and not that? Why this way and not that way? Why this behavior and not that behavior? Why this law and not that law? Why this God and not another? Wonder Woman was right. "The truth is enough. The truth is beautiful."[17]

The truth about the reality of God is vitally important to building a solid foundation for my life and the life to come. Much is at stake. Everything is on the line. In a day and age where the importance of truth in popular culture is diminished (if not completely tossed out) and universal/absolute truth is deemed irrelevant, individualized, and easily dismissed, getting to the truth matters greatly. Moral relativism is of little value. Jeremy Stangroom and Ophelia Benson, editors of *The Philosophy Magazine*, stated in their book *Why Truth Matters*, "We ought to respect the truth, and try to find out what it is, which entails not fudging it whenever we don't like what we find."[18] What is absolutely true can never be altered. It is "always correct, everywhere, all the time, under any condition,"[19] and that also pertains to the reality and truth of God. God matters. I matter, and that makes the search for Him, the Source of all wisdom and truth, a necessity, valuable, and worthy of my finest effort. Should you see and find the reality of God, and you can, *"The (absolute) truth will make you free"* (John 8:32, KJV), so said Jesus — free from worry, stupid decisions, poor values, discouragement, fear, and so much more. All of life is dependent upon revealed truth. Knowing God, *"the way, the truth, and the life"* (John 14:6) will permit you to *"walk on air."* Put the "pixie dust" away. You won't need it. It's not real. It doesn't work.

> *"Never let the noise of this world keep you from hearing the voice of God."*
>
> —Author Unknown

# 8

## GOD BEHIND THE SCENES

God has never missed a day of work. You will find Him in the fields dressed in denim overalls, a checkered flannel shirt with His sleeves rolled up, leather steel-tip boots on His feet, gloves to cover His calloused hands, a rake and shovel slung over His shoulder, and a tool belt strapped to His waist, ready to go to work, planting and harvesting, fixing fences, feeding sheep, and chasing off wolves. He is always working, always doing, always on the move. He just never quits.

A miracle happened the other day. A complete stranger had compassion on me and gave me a ride when I desperately needed one. I was seated in McDonald's having lunch and suddenly realized as I was getting up to leave that I had misplaced my car keys. I searched everywhere — pant pockets, jacket, the floor under the table, the men's room, even the parking lot, but couldn't find them. They were nowhere to be found. I panicked. Another set was nearly four miles away, and I had no way of retrieving them other than walking down a four-lane, busy highway. But God was on the job. A man in the booth next to me, who I did not know, must have noticed my frantic search and came to my rescue, permitting me to disrupt his lunch and daily routine. He offered to taxi me from the restaurant and back again to secure another set of keys. On the way, I thanked him and expressed my gratitude for his help. He turned to me and said, "God put us here to help one another." I wanted to hug him. Imagine, a Christian man being placed in my life at that precise moment when I needed support and assistance — a warm, kind, gentle-spirited man willing to step into the life of a stranger and help. Go figure. That's a miracle. That is God working behind the scenes, sending me one of His very own to get me out of a jam and teach me again of God's faithfulness. Heaven seems to make a habit of doing just that — coming to my rescue, resolving problems, building trust, and helping me to grow in my faith.

I got an unexpected call late one morning from a man who had been walking down Main Street in a small town in upstate New York, when he noticed an old church building. At the time, I was the senior pastor of that little church. He got my name and phone number from the signage in front of the building and so called me. I was getting ready to leave our home with the family to travel to Grandma and Grandpa's for the day. I was literally walking out the door when the phone rang three or four times. I wasn't going to answer it, but my wife insisted, "I think you should get that." It turned out to be good advice.

I picked up the phone, and the man introduced himself. He was in town looking to give away some property for tax purposes and felt led (we had a hunch as to Who was leading him) to gift the house and all its contents to the church. He had never lived in the community, nor had he ever attended our church, or met me, or anyone else from our congregation for that matter. In fact, we had never spoken before his phone call that morning. He also had no knowledge of our need for a new worship center and the decision made some months ago to take on a building project, since the old church was in disrepair. We were a small congregation and wondering how the new facility was going to be financed, but we pressed ahead confident of God's leading and provision. God always finances His plans, a principle we learned to live by.

"As dawn rises over Marble Head" (that's me), I finally saw "the light," a divine opportunity, and asked the man, whose name escapes me, "Where are you?" He responded, "I am standing outside the church on Main Street." I said, "Stay there! I'll be right down." I put my plans aside and allowed God to interrupt my day to introduce me to a man I later came to see as God's emissary, delivering God's message that the property, a three-story house and all its contents, was to be deeded to the church. The money generated from that transaction provided the necessary funds to proceed with the building project and complete it without a mortgage or debt — an unexpected glimpse of the God Who had been working all along behind the scenes to complete His plans. Coincidence? Not a chance! Jesus said, *"My Father is always at His work to this very day, and I too am working"* (John 5:15 (NIV).

The work of God never ceases, staying focused at all times on getting the best results for my daily life. He is always pressing me forward, looking to perfectly fit the various parts of my life together, like "a thousand-piece puzzle," until the picture of His perfect plan for me (and you) is complete and comes to fruition. God has a holy agenda, a sacred objective for my life, a divine blueprint to follow, and He will see it through to completion in ways I never could have anticipated or imagined. Paul wrote, *"I am certain that God, who began the good work within you, will continue his work until it is finally finished..."* (Philippians 1:6, NLT).

Joseph, the son of Jacob, was a kid with dreams and ambitions. He was the apple of his father's eye, and his brothers hated him for it, and with good reason. He was a prideful, young, immature man who boasted often of his future, which included a position of authority over his brothers that they found rather distasteful and hard to accept. Eventually, they'd had enough of his bragging and hatched a plan to rid themselves of the boy. They sold him into slavery, and he ended up in Potiphar's household as a servant to an Egyptian family. Later, he was falsely accused of attempted rape and thrown into prison for years, an innocent man incarcerated for something he didn't do. He was without hope.

I don't know what Joseph was thinking or feeling during the years he stared outside the bars of his cell, but my reaction would have been to cry "foul, unfair, wrong! This is not how my story is supposed to go. This is not what I envisioned for myself. These are not my dreams, my ambitions, or my plans." This sounds all too familiar to me.

Joseph's life had gone from bad to worse, from promising to pathetic, from hopeful to hopeless, feeling like maybe he had lost touch with God. But it was not so — *"because God was with him; whatever he did God made sure it worked out for the best"* (Genesis 39:21, MSG).

The truth is that, behind the scenes, God carries out His comprehensive will for my life and yours *"to bestow on them* [those grieving and upset over life] *a crown of beauty instead of ashes, the oil of joy instead of mourning, and a garment of praise instead of a spirit of despair"* (Isaiah 63:3, NIV).

God is at work, positioning the likes of Joseph for greatness to bring about the rescue of his family and that of an entire nation. Who could have written such a script? His life had become a series of unexpected twists and turns (like most of ours), but each event and situation (even the hard ones) were divinely designed and necessary to make Joseph (and the rest of us) highly useful and productive in bringing about God's perfect will and good plans. God whispers in my pain and confusion, *"I know what I'm doing. I have it all planned out — plans to take care of you, not abandon you, plans to give you the future you hope for"* (Jeremiah 29:11, MSG). That is our daily hope — finding a miracle-working God intervening, interfering, and interceding on our behalf, whether we immediately see it or not — a principle I'd do well to latch on to more firmly.

Mrs. Crawley (of Downton Abbey fame), the grandmother with a sharp intellect and an even sharper tongue (one of my favorite characters in the award-winning series), is pictured talking with a former Russian prince she had met years ago — a man who had known difficult and troublesome days. He had been through a bloody revolution and spent time in a hellish prison, but had recently found his way to England. Now a free man, the prince spoke of courage and hope for a better tomorrow. Mrs. Crawley responded sarcastically with razor-sharp words, "Hope is but a tease to keep us from accepting reality." A depressing worldview, to say the least. There is a better perspective, centered in the reality of God and finding Him, trusting Him, and following Him every day. *"The Lord is with you...Go in this your strength"* (Judges 6:14). There is nothing more real than God.

At the close of his life, with his grandchildren at his feet, Joseph's father looked back over the years, surveying the events and sometimes painful experiences that made up his earlier days, and came to this conclusion, *"God...has been my shepherd all my life to this day"* (Genesis 48:15). That's no tease. That's reality. That is hope. That's an acknowledgement of the presence of God in his life and mine. Israel's eyesight was poor due to old age, but he could clearly see the hand of God at work throughout the years. I suspect you could, too, though at times the vision of God's work behind the scenes is often blurred and my spiritual sight is limited at best, especially in times of uncertainty and doubt.

Under the stress of war and botched battles, an anxious, discouraged, scared Gideon complained bitterly, *"If the Lord is with us* [as I had been told], *why then has all this happened to us* [me]? *And where are all His miracles which our fathers told us about?"* (Judges 6:13). A fair enough question I've asked on more than one occasion. What Gideon didn't know about the work of God, and what I often forget, is that "it may be precisely in the moments we understand Him [God] the least that He is working the most...what we thought were setbacks were God's setups all along."[1]

In the end, Gideon did the smart thing. He sought after God, found Him, talked things over with Him, and was empowered by Him to put God's word and plan to the test, leading three hundred men to victory over an enemy as *"numerous as the sand on the seashore"* (Judges 7:12). God was working behind the scenes in and through Gideon to rid Israel of the Midianites who had threatened and harassed the people for seven long years. But nobody saw it, including the man himself. Nobody saw what God was doing or that He was doing anything at all. Their lands were overrun, and their wealth and livelihood stolen right out from under them. Not surprisingly, they were *"brought very low,"* emotionally drained of all resolve, depressed and discouraged — *"the sons of Israel cried to the Lord on account of Midian"* (Judges 6:7). I've done a good bit of crying to the Lord myself. For Gideon, there was no sense of the presence of God or of His plan to rescue Israel from their enemies, only an overwhelming despair. They found the problems (we're pretty good at that), but failed to see God's promises and the reality of His presence.

The real issue is that most of us (including myself) walk by sight more often than we do by faith and wonder why we end up depressed, unhappy, feeling useless, woeful and desperate, crying to the Lord, over the way things should be, but aren't. Our physical eyes may be sharp and clear, but our spiritual eyes are "dim." Hannah Whitall Smith, made this remark in her book, *The God of All Comfort*:

---

*…the religious life of most of us [is] full of discomfort and unrest. In fact, it seemed, as one of my Christian friends said to me one day when we were comparing our experiences, "as if we had just enough religion to make us miserable."*[2]

---

An honest appraisal. The religious life is "miserable." A life lived in relationship with God is an entirely different matter.

God is not into rolling the dice when it comes to our personal lives. He does not fumble around with luck. There is no such thing in His economy. He has ordered our days. *"The Lord directs the steps of the godly. He delights in every detail of their lives"* (Psalm 37:23). He knows what He wants, and then sets in motion a plan for us that cannot fail and will maximize our abilities to get the best results for His kingdom and ultimately bring the greatest amount of joy, satisfaction, and contentment to our lives at day's end. Know with absolute certainty that God is at work behind the scenes. He is up to something, and it is always something good in the long run.

Paul wrote to the church at Thessalonica that he wanted to visit them. It never materialized. He stated that he was *"eager with great desire to see [them]."* On more than one occasion, he tried to make the journey, but *"Satan thwarted [hindered] me"* (I Thessalonians 2:17–18), he said. That was the way Paul saw it. Satan stood in his way. He impeded Paul's progress, frustrated his plans, and would not permit the Apostle to get to where he wanted to go. On the surface, it appeared that Satan had gotten the upper hand and Paul was forced to remain in place (possibly at Corinth), unsure of his next step. He didn't fully understand God's plan in all this, but he knew that an omniscient God worked with a higher purpose in mind and had things under divine control. Nothing is happenstance in God's rule, though none of us have immediate access to all the details and the meaning behind every event and circumstance God permits. Consequently, I do still have questions, like you, surrounding the power and plans of Heaven's Sovereign. Could anything or anyone (including all the powers of Hell) thwart the will of almighty God and disrupt His plans? Is there any power on earth and in the heavens and beyond that can buck up against God and put a halt to whatever it is He wants to do? The answer is abundantly clear. Nothing or no one can stand in God's way. The sovereign God of the universe, the King of the ages is going to get what He wants. The lordship and wisdom of God are at work behind the scenes and directly involved in every aspect of a man/woman's daily life, right down to the smallest of details, no matter how easy or hard the circumstances. Likewise, God ignored Paul's desire to visit the Thessalonians for reasons unknown to the Apostle at the time. God had a plan that neither Paul nor the devil and his hordes of demons were privy to. Their vision was clouded. They never saw the specifics of God's primary goal. Nobody does, at least not completely, not in this life. God's plan and ultimate purpose remained hidden. John Walvoord, former president of Dallas Seminary, used to say that "One should not try to unscrew the inscrutable." Counsel worth considering. Think of it.

If Paul had ever gotten his own way and showed up for a Wednesday night prayer meeting at the church in Thessalonica, the Apostle may never have sat down to write. There would be no need. However, before the first stroke of his pen, God earmarked Paul's letters to influence and encourage the generations to come and countless numbers of people to faithfully follow Christ. From the start, God intended Paul's letters to reach beyond northern Greece. They were meant to expand the borders of God's kingdom across the globe and prepare the saints throughout history for the coming of *"the day of the Lord"* (I Thessalonians 5:2), to challenge followers of Christ from every age to walk daily with God, and ultimately to impact eternity and fill Heaven — the very reason Paul *had* to write. Obviously, God had much bigger plans in mind (He usually does), wanting to accomplish more than Paul or the Thessalonians could ever have imagined. God was at work well beyond the immediate need, and nobody could fathom the divine end game, not Satan, not Paul, no one, and that includes you and me.

So often, I can't quite figure out what God's up to in the details of my life, where He's taking me and for what reason. Not an uncommon problem, but certainly an uncomfortable one. Yet God always has something in mind, something my finite eyes are unable to see or anticipate, especially when things are not going the way I want. Nonetheless, I am to seek Him out, find Him, get in step with Him (wherever that may lead), trust Him, and follow Him…even if I have no idea at the time what it all means. Though I continue to struggle with uncertainty, the one thing I do know for sure, I'm part of the divine scheme (as you are), and it's a good one. Now, it may not seem so good at the moment, but His plan and purpose are worth pursuing. Like Paul, I may be surprised by God's methods, but I'll be amazed at all He has in store for *"those who love [Him and] are called according to His purpose"* (Romans 8:28). God gets results.

I had a t-shirt made for my granddaughter some years ago when she was facing troubling days and the disappointments of unfulfilled dreams. It simply read, "Walk with the King. He will take you places you once thought impossible." I still believe that to be true, not only for her but for the rest of us who follow Christ, as well. My life is a testimony to that very fact, and I suspect, so is yours, or at least it will be.

After four years of military service during the Vietnam War, I was discharged in December of 1971. The next month, I was enrolled in seminary preparing for the pastoral ministry. I had a wife and a daughter and hardly a penny to my name. I really had no idea how we would make it financially. Between daily living expenses (food, rent, utilities, etc.) and tuition and books, the prospects seemed a bit dim. I knew only one thing — God had called me to His service and to attend Gordon-Conwell Theological Seminary. I had the GI Bill to help pay for educational and living expenses, but it wasn't enough. I had to trust Him for the remainder. There was no other option. I learned very quickly that God always comes through — somewhat of a cliché, but nonetheless true. My wife found a part-time job and worked for three years to help put me through school. I worked at a local church on the weekends for a small stipend. But things remained tight. One day I went to the mailbox and found an envelope. There was no return address and no familiar postmark. I had no idea who it was from. I opened it. No note — just sixty dollars in cash. I was stunned. God's provision. God's faithfulness. God working behind the scenes. The money continued for nearly three years, month after month, until graduation day. And then like manna from heaven, it stopped when it was no longer needed, and we were on our way to our first church assignment. All bills paid in full. No loans. No debt. We never found out who was helping us, but we knew Who was behind it all.

I recall driving a U-Haul van north up 9W in New York State with what little we owned. We were heading to First Baptist to begin our ministry with a small congregation that recently suffered a church split and was left with approximately twelve active members. Needless to say, the salary was small, and the denomination had to kick in a significant amount of funding to keep the church doors open and help in the support of a young pastor and his family. We had few possessions, very little furniture (certainly insufficient to fill a three-bedroom house), twenty-six dollars in my pocket, and a wife and child in tow, and I wondered again how we were going to survive. I should have known.

When we arrived at the parsonage, the place we would call home for the next fifteen years, the people were there waiting to welcome us. We walked into the kitchen. The pantry was filled. The refrigerator was loaded. The freezer was stocked. One church member invited me to come down to his furniture store the next day and pick out whatever we wanted and needed. We had so little, but God knew. He went before us and made a way where there was no way…always working behind the scenes to see His perfect plans come to pass.

The most important decision I ever made was to follow God. He has never failed me, nor has He ever left me to fend for myself. He is always working His best for my best.

*"Often I have not known where I was going until I was already there. I have had my share of desires and goals, but my life has come to me, or I have gone to it mainly by way of mistakes and surprises. Often I have received better than I deserved. Often my faintest hopes have rested on bad mistakes. I am an ignorant pilgrim, crossing a dark valley. And yet for a long time, looking back, I have been unable to shake off the feeling that I have been led—make of that what you will."*

—Jayber Crow
(from the novel by Wendell Berry)[1]

# 9

## HE LEADETH ME

I was heading out on a recruiting trip to Raleigh, North Carolina, and a showcase tournament for high school soccer players wanting to play at the collegiate level. My plane was delayed in Chattanooga and then canceled due to the weather. I was going to miss my connecting flight. I was frustrated. I had a plan and a timetable, but nothing seemed to be working out to my satisfaction. The airlines rebooked me on a different carrier, departing to a different city, at a different time, and changed my seat assignments. I was annoyed and wondering if I would ever get to my destination, as originally planned. I should have realized that God was up to something, leading me down a path of His own choosing.

I made my connections. Got to my gate. Entered the plane and walked down the aisle searching for my seat number. I found it. Placed my bags overhead and sat down. It was an aisle seat. I looked at the passenger next to me peering out the window. He was an older teen, a strong, athletic, handsome, young Mexican man from Texas. I also took notice of an athletic bag pushed under the seat in front of him. I introduced myself and asked if he was a soccer player heading to the Raleigh tournament. Much to my surprise, he indicated that he was and that he was looking for a college that offered a business major and that would provide the opportunity to play men's soccer. He admitted, "I don't know what I'm doing or how to get connected with college coaches." I informed him that I was a college coach and was headed to the tournament in search of student athletes who were academically qualified and able to play at the next level. I said, "I will help you. I'll do what I can to see that you are in the place of God's choosing, even if it is not with my team. I'll come watch you play, give you an assessment of your abilities, and provide you the information you need to make an informed decision." Then it hit me.

God had engineered our meeting. Our entire day had been orchestrated by Him. He seems to like doing that a lot. God put us together, got us on the same airplane, with the same carrier, at the same time, going to the same place, and parked us in the same row with adjoining seats, both in God's place in God's time, two people from different countries and cities, and varying backgrounds — a coach from Dayton, Tennessee, searching for players and an anxious young man from Mexico looking to find his future. Unknown to either of us, God had taken us by the hand and led us to cross paths and meet at this point in our lives. "Son," I said, "I don't know where you are spiritually, or even whether you believe in God, but there is no doubt in my mind that we are obviously on a divine appointment. This is no accident, nor coincidence. God has led us here and brought us together. Let's follow His lead and see where all this goes." Incidentally, he came to Bryan College where he was exposed to the claims of Christ, got a Christian education, a degree in business, baptized in a local church, and played four years for me. He had a stellar career.

In 1862, John H. Gilmore wrote a song whose words are as true today as they were more than a hundred years ago.

---

### Verse One
*He leadeth me, O blessed thought! O words with heav'nly comfort fraught! Whate'er I do, where'er I be, Still 'tis God's hand that leadeth me.*

### Refrain
*He leadeth me, He leadeth me, By His own hand He leadeth me; His faithful foll'wer I would be, For by His hand He leadeth me.*

### Verse Two
*Lord, I would place my hand in Thine, Nor ever murmur nor repine; Content, whatever lot I see, Since 'tis my God that leadeth me.*

---

Gilmore later gave the historical context of this hymn and indicated his dependence on the Twenty-Third Psalm.

---

*It was the darkest hour of the Civil War. I did not refer to that fact—that is, I don't think I did—but it may subconsciously have led me to realize that God's leadership is the one significant fact in human experience, that it makes no difference how we are led, or whither we are led, so long as we are sure God is leading us.*[2]

---

Having lost nearly everything of genuine value (health, family, and livelihood) in a series of catastrophic, unexplained events, Job weighed out his prior experience with God and what he had learned over the years about the character of God. He gathered his evidence as in a courtroom and confidently stood before the Judge of the universe to present His case. He was a man of character and integrity. God Himself said Job was *"a blameless and upright man, fearing God and turning away from evil"* (Job 1:8), and yet God permitted the testing his faith and commitment. Lesser men might have broken under the strain of unexpected trials, but Job stood his ground and continued to follow God's leading. In the end, Job's life became a demonstration for the whole world to see just how a person can successfully keep the faith under extreme pressure, handle life's disappointments, heartache and grief, and stand tall when *"darkness and black gloom claim"* (Job 3:5) the day. Job did what he had always done in good times and bad. *"He fell to the ground and worshiped"* (Job 1:20) an act of undeniable, deep commitment and abandonment to the will of God, come what may. I got the memo. *"The Lord gave, and the Lord has taken away; blessed be the name of the Lord"* (Job 1:21, ESV) — "Content, whatever lot I see, Since 'tis my God that leadeth me."

R. Kirby Godsey, who served twenty-seven years as President and CEO of Mercer University, reminded us of this:

> *The Christian faith is about finding a new center from which to see and understand our world, even when agony and ugliness are abundant. If we are simply in search of an easy fix for the pain, the Christian faith is not likely to be much help…(but it does offer) a pathway toward strength and wisdom and hope…(and) teaches us that failure and loss should never become the defining essence of our lives.*[3]

Billy Sunday lived in a small cabin in Iowa. The family struggled with poverty and the early death of his father. Life had become harsh and unforgiving. Unable to handle the strain of a second marriage gone bad, his mother abandoned Billy and left him at the Soldier's Orphans Home. There baseball became his passion and soon he developed the skills necessary to play professionally for the Chicago White Stockings in 1883, no doubt a rags-to-riches story. Some years later, Sunday visited the Pacific Garden Mission in Chicago, where he met Christ and was called by God to leave the baseball diamond behind and proclaim the gospel, "inviting people to 'walk the sawdust trail'…to indicate their decision for Christ."[4] A man of passion, conviction, and the guts to speak the Word of God with boldness, without compromise, and with clarity. "I want to preach the gospel so plainly," he said, "that men can come from the factories and not have to bring a dictionary."[5] And he did just that. Sunday found a "new center" — God Himself — and refused to let the heartaches of the past define his future. "He leadeth me" to speak and live the truth.

God led a country boy named Billy Graham from the hills of North Carolina, to make him one of the most effective and respected evangelists the world has ever seen, traveling the globe to proclaim the gospel of grace and the mercy of God to presidents, kings and queens, and to more than eighty million common, everyday people. He founded *Christianity Today* and the *Hour of Decision* magazines to promote faith in Christ and successful Christian living. Graham lived an extraordinary life driven by a remarkable love for God and a willingness to serve His interests.[6] God led him to the pulpits of America and beyond and to the great stadiums across the world. God used him in ways no one could have ever imagined or predicted — a life and ministry directed by God from the very start to show the world what He can do with a man who dares to answer the call of God and follow His lead, a good decision by any standard that will most certainly impact this life for the better and the life to come. God would do the same for any man or woman who would *"first and most importantly seek [aim at, strive after] His kingdom and His righteousness [doing and being right], and all these things will be given to you also* (Matthew 6:33, AMP). The most important priority in life is to seek God. Go where you must, as often as you must, again and again if necessary, until you find

Christ…and you will find Him, because He first found you. He has already made Himself known to every generation, and wants you to discover His grace and mercy. He wants you to see and experience His power to conquer life, hear Him speak into your life, and then follow Him wherever He leads, even to the ends of the world.

God latched onto a young man named John Bunyan, a penniless traveling tinker, who by his own admission, "had but few equals, both for cursing, swearing, lying, and blaspheming the holy name of God" (quite a resume). But the hand of God was on his life, leading a rebel to write some of Christendom's best known and influential books during a twelve-year imprisonment, including *Pilgrim's Progress* (which sold 100,000 copies [in his lifetime]).[7] "He leadeth me, O blessed thought!" to "*take [my] everyday, ordinary life — [my] sleeping, eating, going-to-work, and walking-around life — and place it before God as an offering…Readily [recognizing] what He wants from [me], and quickly respond to it*" (Romans 12:1–2, MSG). A very good decision not to be delayed.

God reached into a "crazy rock band" (Korn) and into the life of a young man who spent most of his days "partying like a wild man" — Brian "Head" Welch, lead guitarist for Korn and "a very depressed lost soul" (his words, not mine). God led him out of a self-abusive, sensual, dark, and hapless life, where he did a lot of "the stupid things,"[8] and brought him to the foot of the cross. There God mercifully nailed his pain, anger, hopelessness, loneliness, "inner demons," moral failures and shame to the cross of Christ, where the Son of God bled down love, forgiveness, and grace — forever changing the man's life. Miraculously free of his past, God allowed Brian to serve Him with his talents and the testimony of his personal and public life. Brian relates this:

> *I'm just thankful that I have a story with Christ. I've been telling the story for fifteen years in one way or another…I'm authentic…my faith is deep…I'm really walking this out…God has taken every bad thing I went through and turned it around*

> *for good. That's just what He does…And if He did that for me, He'll do it for anybody.*⁹

And so it goes. "He leadeth me, O blessed thought…" right to the cross.

Feeling the shame of his own sin and a past riddled with moral lapses (much like the rest of us), Peter bowed low before the Lord. *"Depart from me for I am a sinful man"* (Luke 5:8) was the cry of his dubious heart, at least that was how he felt and how I've often felt about myself, a convicted spiritual felon. Sin forces me to see what I truly am and where I've been. Peter saw the problem — his sin and shortcomings and flaws; Jesus saw his potential and his future promise, and would not give up on him. God would not and did not write off the man as useless and unredeemable, and He didn't do that with me, for God sees what I *can be*, where I *can go*, and what I *can do* in the days ahead. In the eyes of God, I am much more than I think, much more than my past. In fact, my past is no indication of what I can become in the future. In God's economy, my past does not define me. God had something better for Peter (and for me and you). So, He picked the man up, dusted him off, and led him to the cross, the place where all of us must go, and sometimes return again and again, day after day, moment by moment. The cross is the place where:

- Forgiveness is found on Calvary's hill outside Jerusalem and nowhere else in this vast universe.

- Forgiveness is firmly secured, mercifully offered, and made possible in Christ and Christ alone.

- Forgiveness *"takes away [my] sin"* (John 1:29) for all time and eternity.

- Forgiveness flows down from above to reach, redeem, rescue, and restore undeserving men and women, of whom I am one.

- Forgiveness is made possible because the justice of God is fully satisfied and my guilt is removed *"as far as the east is from the west"* (Psalm 103:12).

- Forgiveness promises me a future when I had none (cf. Hebrews 10:17).

The cross is the place where I must choose — the most important, life-changing, transforming decision "anybody" can make — to journey with Christ by the grace of God or go my own way.

The journey to find and follow God's leading is no "cakewalk." No easy road. No quiet walk in the park. It is a "wild" trek through uncharted trails, winding unmarked roads, over mountains and valleys, and into remote and barren places at a frightening pace. Jesus said of His own journey and ours:

> **John 12:24–25, TPT** – *Let me make this clear: A single grain of wheat will never be more than a single grain of wheat unless it drops into the ground and dies (the man/woman who abandons his/her own will to follow God). Because then it sprouts and produces a great harvest of wheat—all because one grain died. The person who loves his life and pampers himself will miss true life! But the one who detaches his life from this world and abandons himself to me, will find true life and enjoy it forever.*

I think I prefer a much calmer, predictable, and more civilized path to follow (how boring) and escape the "wild" places God would take me to discover His purpose for my life. That journey can be extremely difficult and challenging, sometimes taking me through the wilderness, but it culminates in *"the promise land,"* at the place of God's choosing, where the follower of Christ will experience the reality of redemption, the mercy and peace of God, and a new meaning and plan for living.

After Terah (Abram's father) died in Haran, Abram was directed by God to pull up his tent pegs, pack up his tents, and leave town. Remarkedly, he did just that, having no idea where he was going, only that he was heading by faith (cf. Hebrews 11:8) *"to the land"* which God promised to show him and give him (cf. Genesis 12:1), *"a good land…a land flowing with milk and honey"* (Exodus 3:8, ESV). There Abram's name would become great, a nation would be built from the ground up, and the world would benefit from his decision to obey and follow God's leading. Talk about a wild ride for a seventy-five-year-old man! Abraham's journey of faith was significant, and the life principles learned along the way are noteworthy and applicable to my daily life and walk with God. Here are several gleaned from the life of a man who stepped forward to follow God's leading.

- I don't need all the questions answered prior to obeying and following through on God's leading and calling to move forward. Better to "Just do it!" like the Nike slogan suggests.

- God has a plan for my life, designed and laid out in eternity past that I must find, learn to trust, and follow, if I want the best for my life.

- The call of God was/is both personal and purposeful. I have a significant role to play in God's schemes.

- God often requires a man/woman to sever ties with the past. Leave yesterday behind and move on to something new, fully orchestrated by God.

- God often takes me out of my comfort zone (away from country, relatives/family, home, friends, etc.) to previously unknown territory and adventures well beyond my ability to imagine.

- Life is built upon the sure Word of God. I can stake my life on His instructions and press forward with confidence.

- God majors in that which seems impossible, leading me into situations that frequently require me to rely on Him.

- Faith and trust are necessary in responding to the call of God to follow Him.

- Stay focused on God's plan. Don't get sidetracked on the trivial and unimportant, chasing things that don't matter. The shortest distance between two points is a straight line!

- God desires for me to know His will for my life. He does not play hide-n-seek with any person who is truly open to God's direction and leading.

- The blessing of God is contingent on me not staying where I am, but on my willingness to follow the imperative, "Go forth!" and move as God directs.

- The going MUST follow the calling — *"So Abram went forth as the Lord had spoken to him"* (Genesis 12:4).

- Obedience is required to get the most out of what God desires to do (cf. Genesis 12:2–3) in my daily life.

- The call of God is bigger and greater than my plans could ever be. He wants to do more in and through my life than I ever thought possible.

Mike Lindell is "an ordinary guy from Minnesota," the My Pillow man, once a cocaine and alcohol addict with a heavy gambling problem, lonely and broke, a failure as a husband and father. His life was a wreck,[10] but God led him out of "a life spent running from, and then running to, the God of second and third and fourth chances. It is the story of a God who is in the business of redeeming sin and failure with grace."[11]

In every story, only two true options are available across the spectrum of daily experiences. Follow Christ or try some other path. Either you yell in the streets with a rebellious crowd, *"Away with Him [Jesus]"* (John 19:15), or you plead for your life along with the thief, *"Jesus, remember me when You come in Your kingdom"* (Luke 23:42). The choice has remained ours since we walked the green, lush gardens of Eden — peace of mind and heart, or spiritual unrest and emotional turmoil. Trust Him with the specifics of your daily life, or shun God and dare to figure things out on your own. Rely on Him and His wisdom and counsel to direct your affairs and actions or lean on your own understanding and judgments, neither of which may get you too far in this life. Follow His lead, or dig your feet in and stubbornly refuse to get in step with His directions. The decision to pursue God or not will be the most important decision you will ever make.

> *"All you need is love. But a little chocolate now and then doesn't hurt."*[1]
>
> —Charles Schulz

# 10

## THE LOVE OF MY LIFE

In 90 A.D., John the Apostle wrote a letter to the churches near Ephesus. His theme, *"love comes from God. Everyone who loves has been born of God and knows God…because God is love"* is as relevant today as at any time in human history. Love underscores all of life, and "a little chocolate" will go a long way in our relationships with others and with God.

Love is not simply strong affection or attraction. I have that for a slice of pizza and apple crumb cheesecake. It is not just about "warm fuzzy feelings," though emotions are important in the short term and do play a limited role in relationships. However, goose bumps won't last long. Starry eyes get misty and restrict vision. Sweating palms become damp and clammy. Love songs are soppy, at best. Romantic love, as fun and exciting as it is, does not cut it over the long haul. And love certainly is not "never having to say I'm sorry," an idea made popular by the 1970 movie, *Love Story*. Love is more, much more.

A group of professionals asked a group of four to eight year olds, "What does love mean?" The answers they received were profound, down-to-earth, right on the money, and amazingly practical. Adults sit up and take note. I could not possibly improve on their insights. Here are several:

- "Love is when Mommy sees Daddy smelly and sweaty and still says he is handsomer than Robert Redford."

- "Love is when you go out to eat and give somebody most of your French fries without making them give you any of theirs."

- "When someone loves you, the way they say your name is different. You just know that your name is safe in their mouth."

- "Love is like a little old woman and a little old man who are still friends even after they know each other so well."

- "During my piano recital I was on a stage, and I was scared. I looked at all the people watching me and saw my daddy waving and smiling. He was the only one doing that. I wasn't scared anymore."

- A four-year-old child had a next door neighbor, an elderly gentleman who had recently lost his wife. Upon seeing the man cry, the little boy went into the old gentleman's yard, climbed onto his lap, and just sat there. When his Mother asked what he had said to the neighbor, the little boy said, "'Nothing, I just helped him cry."[2]

Insightful and moving.

R.C. Sproul wrote:

> *Whatever else God's love is...[it] is characterized by the qualities that define holiness — transcendence and purity. First, God's love is transcendent...set apart and different from everything we experience in creation. Second, God's love is pure.*

> *His love is absolutely flawless, having no selfishness, wickedness, or sin mixed in with it. God's love is not ordinary or profane. It is a majestic, sacred love that goes far beyond anything creatures can manifest…The love of God is in a class by itself…it is a love that He shares in part with us and expects us to manifest it to each other.*[3]

Real love is action, a deliberate calculated act — a decision to do, support, extend a helping hand to fallen people, and a commitment to wanting the best for someone else, even at great personal cost. Love is listening to the heartbeat of another and dreaming big dreams alongside them, wiping away tears when life hurts, laughing together at silly things, binding up wounds, moving through the day with mercy and compassion. It is gracious without conditions or qualifications, like God Himself. Love is sacrifice, surrender, laying down your life, remaining vulnerable, for love is always risky. Love is God remaining fully committed to our well-being and success whether we deserve it or not. The love of God is selfless and generous and full of grace and truth. "Love," wrote G.K. Chesterton, " means loving the unlovable." To love is to rejoice in the strengths and abilities, gifts and talents of others. It overlooks faults, covers up failures, and forgives without strings attached. No grudges. No negotiations. No preconditions. No middle ground. And for heaven's sake, no finger-pointing…ever. Warts and imperfections included, accepting people where they are and as they are. Love is persistent, reaching out, rescuing, and lifting up, dusting off, and then starting all over again each day, and again, and again. Love is all in! It is how God loves you and me day in and day out, through the ups and downs, in the disappointments and in the thrill that accompanies victory, always and forever, till the stars drop from the sky and the mountains crumble to dust. *"Love never fails,"* so said the Apostle Paul to the church at Corinth (cf. I Corinthians 13:8). "We should be astonished at the goodness of God," wrote Brennan Manning, "stunned that He should bother to call us by name, our mouths wide open at His love, bewildered that at this very moment we are standing on holy ground."[4]

Love is the very character of God. He is love; John told us that. He gave it a name, agape love — a love that holds me and you in the highest regard, that sees great value in each one of us, and regards my relationship with God Himself as the most important factor and highest priority in daily life. Love divine is never cautious, but vigilant and aggressive, reaching beyond itself, doing whatever it takes to enter into my miserable state, into the fallen affairs of my life, pull me to my feet, reorient my perspective on what's truly important, and then sends me off on a new course toward successful living to get the most out of this life and the life to come.

That's the God I want to pursue and find. That's the God I want to see when I roll out of bed in the morning, when I am jobless, without a roof over my head, when a bottle of whiskey is my sole comfort, when my spouse has decided to pack up her things and walk out the door, or when guilt and shame overwhelm my soul. In the good times and the hard times, I need the sure love of God to envelope me, sustain me, and take me to a better place than I am right now. This is the God I need to love me when I'm lying in a hospital bed alone sick as a dog, wondering if I'm ever going to get home again, or when I need money for college, and I have none.

Timothy Harrison arrived at the local Waffle House in Center Point, Alabama, and clocked in to start his shift for the day, the day of his high school graduation at Woodlawn. But he was not going. Times were tough for the young man. He had no cap and gown, no graduation tickets, no dress clothes, and no ride across town to get to the ceremony. Cedric Hampton, Harrison's manager at Waffle House, was surprised to see him.

"Why aren't you going to graduation?"

Harrison responded, "I don't want to miss work." He couldn't afford to do otherwise.

"You're going!" Hampton replied.

Harrison's coworkers stopped everything, banded together, and went into action, committed to see their friend succeed and experience the best of life. It is how God's love operates. Harrison's life was about to change. His colleagues bought him some new clothes appropriate for the occasion, including slacks, a new shirt and a tie, drove twenty miles across town to secure his cap and gown, and then made sure he got to the graduation ceremony. It changed the course of this young man's life. That's what love does.

Timothy had difficulty explaining what he felt like when he got dressed for the ceremony — new clothes and cap and gown for the first time. He said. "That was a different feeling, I don't even know the words. A million dollars? It was the best feeling ever…to know that I have a path to go somewhere? That's something new."

After his story went viral, Lawson State Community College offered him a full scholarship, including books. His manager concluded, "Now he can go to college and figure out what do in his life, and we're gonna help guide him." Such is the love of God in action — giving hope and direction and opportunity, touching and transforming the lives of people for the better. *"For God so loved the world,"* (John 3:16), a love that fills the divine heart and is poured out in abundance. The love of God is serious business.[5]

I'm not ashamed to admit that I need God and I need His love, not just any God, but this God — the One who always has my best interest in mind, the One who always comes through for me, the One who alone has power to save *"everyone who believes"* (cf. Romans 1:16), the God Who is so wildly passionate and concerned for my well-being that He "carries my picture in His wallet."[6] That's the God I must find, get to know, and personally experience. No one else will do!

Richard Stearns of World Vision wrote of nineteen-year-old Ruth who had never met her father, a man who rejected her and deserted the family before she was even born. Both anxious and excited, she arranged to meet her dad, but the man never showed up. She said, "I have never known the love of a father." I fully understand.

Raised in poverty, Ruth was forced to quit school a number of times to work and help support the family. Her dream of one day becoming a lawyer to help abused and discarded women and children like herself would have to wait. She desperately needed help and found it in God, whose love reached down into her pain and disappointments, bandaged her wounded heart, and lifted her head to face life with courage and hope. Against the odds, she finished high school and enrolled in the university in Bolivia to pursue a degree in law. And though her earthly father never stepped forward to embrace his daughter, Ruth found the love of God, the love of her heavenly Father, the Love of her life — "enough [love] to overcome everything." She said, "I don't know how, but I know God is with me. God made me. He has a purpose in my trials" and for every "child of the King…deeply loved by Him."[7]

When Isaac Watts surveyed the cross and realized what it cost God to love him (and the rest of us) so deeply, he drew but one conclusion.

*Were the whole Realm of Nature mine,*
*That were a Present far too small;*
*Love so amazing, so divine,*
*Demands my Soul, my Life, my All.*

God is the "Love of my life," the Lover of my soul, made evident in the shadow of the Old Rugged Cross. There you will *"grasp [just] how wide and long and high and deep is the love of Christ"* (cf. Ephesians 3:17–19, NIV). It is without measure or equal.

A number of years ago, I came across a wonderful story about a father's love. I don't know the author or its source, but it remains for me "A Lesson in Love," and helps me to gain some insight into the love of our heavenly Father for us all.

*I watched intently as my little brother was caught in the act. He sat in the corner of the living room, a pen in one hand and my father's brand-new hymnbook in the other.*

*As my father walked into the room, my brother cowered slightly; he sensed that he had done something wrong. From a distance I could see that he had opened my father's new hymnal and scribbled in it the length and breadth of the first page with a pen. Now, staring at my father fearfully, he and I both waited for his punishment. And as we waited, there was no way we could have known that our father was about to teach us deep and lasting lessons about life and family, lessons that continue to become even clearer through the years.*

*My father picked up his prized hymnal, looked at it carefully, and then sat down, without saying a word. Books were precious to him; he was a clergyman and the holder of several degrees. For him, books were knowledge, and yet he loved his children. What he did next was remarkable. Instead of punishing my brother, instead of scolding or yelling or reprimanding, he sat down, took the pen from my brother's hand, and then wrote in the book himself, alongside the scribbles John had made:*

*"John's work, 1959, age 2. How many times have I looked into your beautiful face and into your warm, alert eyes looking up at me and thanked God for the one who has now scribbled in my new hymnal. You have made the book sacred, as have your brothers and sister to so much of my life."*

This is the very character of God, our loving, heavenly Father, Who looks deep into the eyes of those who have made a mess of everything (that's me and probably you, too), foolishly and deliberately "defacing" the life God has given us with bad behavior and poor decisions. Amazingly, He still loves me. I belong to Him. I am still His son. Even in my personal failures and destructive actions, my life remains "sacred" to Him. With all the "scribbling" I've done, His love is undeterred, unshaken, and undisturbed. His love is true, *"from everlasting to everlasting."*

The most important decision you will ever make is to give your life and heart to the One who loves you most. *"How long will you hesitate between two opinions? If the Lord is God, follow Him"* all the days of your life. Pursue the Love of your life, and you will find that sometimes He throws in a "little chocolate" to sweeten your day.

# EPILOGUE

Thomas A. Dorsey was born in Georgia in 1899, reared in Atlanta, and converted to Christianity in 1926. He became active in Pilgrim Baptist Church in Chicago and served as the church's choir director for some forty years. In 1932, he traveled to St. Louis to sing at a revival. His young wife was home in her last month of pregnancy and unable to make the trip. When Dorsey finished singing and sat down, a young boy delivered a telegram while he was still on the platform. Its message was devastating. It simply read: "Your wife just died." He lost his wife Nettie and his first son during childbirth. He said, "I was lost in grief." He buried them both in the same casket. The man fell apart. His passion for life and the gospel was all but gone, and he left the ministry. Remorse can do that. It kills the heart. "I didn't want to serve Him anymore," he said, "or write gospel songs. I just wanted to go back to that jazz world I once knew so well."[1] But God had other plans for a distraught man in search of his life and the healing of his soul. He needed to find his place once again in this world. He needed to find God.

It happened on a quiet night, alone at his piano. There God found a broken man, and out of his grief and despair, Dorsey penned the following words and set them to music adapted from an old hymn, *Must Jesus Bear the Cross Alone.*

---

*Precious Lord, take my hand,*
*Lead me on, let me stand.*
*I'm tired, I'm weak, I'm alone.*
*Through the storm, through the night*
*Lead me on to the light.*
*Take my hand, precious Lord, lead me home.*

*When my way grows drear, precious Lord, linger near*
*When my light is almost gone.*
*Hear my cry, hear my call,*
*Hold my hand lest I fall,*
*Take my hand, precious Lord, lead me home.*

*When the darkness appears, and the night draws near*
*And the day is past and gone.*
*At the river I stand,*
*Guide my feet, hold my hand,*
*Take my hand, precious Lord, lead me home.*

*Precious Lord, take my hand,*
*Lead me on, let me stand,*
*I'm tired, I'm weak, I'm alone.*
*Through the storm, through the night*
*Lead me on to the light.*
*Take my hand precious Lord, lead me home.*[2]

There is but one real choice for living successfully in this world. Seek God. Find Him. Take His hand…and follow. It will be the most important decision you will ever make.

**Isaiah 41:13, NIV** – *For I am the Lord your God who takes hold of your right hand and says to you, Do not fear; I will help you.*

# ABOUT THE AUTHOR

Sanford "Sandy" Zensen is an ordained Baptist and former Christian & Missionary Alliance minister with twenty plus years' experience in pastoral ministry. In addition, he has served twenty-five years as a professor of Christian studies and a Christian college administrator, continuing to teach as an adjunct professor for two separate institutions. He holds two professional degrees, MDiv and DMin, and a PhD in religion and society.

Sandy is a frequent speaker at churches, men's ministries, college alumni functions, and athletic events. He was the 2014 AGS (Adult and Graduate Studies) commencement speaker at Bryan College (Tennessee). He is the author of two books, *On the Wall with Sword and Trowel: The Challenges and Conflicts of Ministry* (WIPF and Stock, 2019) and *Living Deep in a Shallow World* (WIPF and Stock, 2020), each one receiving five-star reviews. He continues to serve as a member and Sunday school teacher at Stuart Heights Baptist Church, one of the largest Southern Baptist churches in the Chattanooga, Tennessee, area.

# END NOTES

**INTRODUCTION**

[1] C.S. Lewis, *Mere Christianity: A Revised and Amplified Edition*, (New York, NY: HarperOne, 1980), 49.

[2] Parker Reardon, "Dispensationalism 101: part 1 — the difference between dispensational & covenantal theology, *Sharper Iron*, Mar 29, 2017, retrieved from https://sharperiron.org/article/dispensationalism-101-part-1-difference-between-dispensational.

[3] Timothy Keller, *The Prodigal God: Recovering the Heart of the Christian Faith*, (New York, NY: Penguin Group, 2008), 108–109.

[4] A.W. Tozer, *The Knowledge of the Holy*, (New York, NY: HarperCollins, 1961), 3.

[5] St. Augustine, AZ Quotes, retrieved from https://www.azquotes.com/quotes/topics/seeking-god.html.

[6] C.H. Spurgeon (1834–1892), *Longing to Find God*, Sept 14, 1890, retrieved from https://www.biblebb.com/files/spurgeon/2272.htm.

[7] George Mueller, "How To Promote the Glory of God," *The Christian: A Weekly Record of Christian Life, Christian Testimony, and Christian Work*, (London: Morgan and Scott, Feb 10, 1870), 17–18.

[8] Joe Gibbs, *Game Plan for Life*, (Grand Rapid, MI: Zondervan, 2012), 71.

[9] Joseph H. Gilmore, *He Leadeth Me*, Public Domain, 1862.

**CHAPTER 1**

[1] Lewis, *op. cit.*, 86–87.

[2] Kathleen Elkins, "Stephen Curry says the best advice he ever got came from his mom when he was 13 years old," *CNBC: Make it*, Dec 11, 2020, retrieved from https://www.cnbc.com/2019/01/09/stephen-curry-says-the-best-advice-he-ever-got-came-from-his-mom.html#:~:text=Success.

[3] Roy T. Bennett, *The Light in the Heart: Inspirational Thoughts For Living Your Best Life*, (Publisher, Roy T. Bennett, Feb 25, 2016), 61.

⁴ J.I. Packer, *Knowing God*, (Downers Grove, Illinois: Intervarsity, 1973), 18.

⁵ Heather J. Bennett, Beyond the Rapids, (Bloomington, IN, Self-published, 2020), 108.

⁶ Posted on Facebook (March 20210) by John Vermilya, senior pastor of The Tabernacle, (Buckley, MI).

⁷ The Prayer of St. Richard Of Chichester (1197–1253), "May I know you more clearly, Love you more dearly, Follow you more nearly, Day by day," *4dlord*, Jan 1, 2016. Retrieved from https://4dlord.wordpress.com/2016/01/01/may-i-know-you-more-clearly-love-you-more-dearly-follow-you-more-nearly-day-by-day/.

⁸ C.S. Lewis, Sacred Space: Your Daily Prayer Online, a ministry of the Irish Jesuits, retrieved from https://www.sacredspace.ie/Scripture/matthew-1017-22.

⁹ Maria Stenvinkel, What's Your Greatest Fear in Life? 65 Brave Answers from People in 18 Countries, LinkedIn, December 19, 2016, retrieved from https://www.linkedin.com/pulse/whats-your-greatest-fear-life-65-brave-answers-from-18-stenvinkel/.

## CHAPTER 2

¹ An interview with Anthony DeCurtis, writer for Rolling Stone magazine, NBC's *"Today,"* 11-30-01.

² M. Night Shyamalan, *Wide Awake* (Miramax Films, 1998).

³ Norman L. Geisler and William E. Nix, *A General Introduction to the Bible*, (Chicago, Illinois: Moody Press, 1986), 198.

⁴ Cornelius Van Til, My Credo, an essay from *Jerusalem and Athens*, E. R. Greehan editor, (Phillipsburg, New Jersey: P&R Publishing Co., (1980), 3-21, retrieved from https://reformed.org/apologetics/my-credo-by-cornelius-van-til/.

⁵ Barth, Carl, *The Epistle to the Romans*, translated from the 6th Edition by Edwyn C. Hoskyns, (London, United Kingdom: Oxford University Press, 1933), 85.

⁶ Chuck Colson, *The Faith*, (Grand Rapids, Michigan: Zondervan, 2008), 93.

⁷ J.D. Greear, Will People Die for a Lie?, J.D. Greear Ministries, May 28, 2019, retrieved from https://jdgreear.com/will-people-die-for-lie/.

⁸ Christian History Magazine Editorial Staff; Mark Galli, Ted Olsen, and J.I. Packer, *131 Christians Everybody Should Know*, (Nashville: TN: B&H Publishing Group, 2000), 68, 76. (Kindle Edition).

⁹ Fred Mendrin and Emily Greene, Prisoner B28545: How A Drug Addict Became A Hardcore Criminal Behind Bars, *Prison Fellowship Blog: In-Prison Stories*, June 7,

2021, retrieved from https://www.prisonfellowship.org/category/in-prison-ministry-2/in-prison-stories/.

[10] Peter S. Williams, *Digging for Evidence*, (London, Great Britain: Christian Evidence Society, 2016), 6.

[11] Geisler and Nix, *op. cit.*, 385.

[12] Randall Price, Handbook of Biblical Archeology, (Grand Rapids, Michigan: Zondervan, 2017), 15.

[13] Hannah Whitall Smith Quotes, Goodreads, retrieved from https://www.goodreads.com/author/quotes/72501.Hannah_Whitall_Smith.

[14] Quotes on Prayer (D.L. Moody), ACTS 413 Ministry, retrieved from https://www.acts413.net/quotes.

[15] Ann Rodgers, Ecuadoran tribe transformed after killing of 5 missionaries, Post-Gazette, N\Jan 7, 2006, retrieved from https://www.post-gazette.com/ae/movies/2006/01/08/Ecuadoran-tribe-transformed-after-killing-of-5-missionaries/stories/200601080177.

[16] 20 Powerful Jim Elliot Quotes, Leadership Resources, Oct 19, 2013, retrieved from https://www.leadershipresources.org/blog/christian-missionary-jim-elliot-quotes/.

[17] Os Guinness, *The Call*, (Nashville, TN: Thomas Nelson, 1998), 4.

[18] Jim Denney, JRR Tolkien, the star of Bethlehem, and the fairy-story that came true, *Fox News*, Dec 24, 2012, retrieved from https://www.foxnews.com/opinion/jrr-tolkien-the-star-of-bethlehem-and-the-fairy-story-that-came-true.

## CHAPTER 3

[1] Aaron Sorkin, A Few Good Men, Castle Rock Entertainment Production Company, Dec 11, 1992.

[2] Nathan J. Stone, Names of God in the Old Testament, (Chicago, Illinois: Moody Press, 1944), 7.

[3] Lori Thomason, "He's Alive," *Pure Devotion*, March 2018, retrieved from https://lthomason.wordpress.com/2018/03/27/living-god/.

[4] C.S. Lewis, *The Inspirational Writings of C.S. Lewis*, (New York, NY: Inspirational Press, 1994), 125.

[5] Os Guinness and John Seel, *No God but God*, (Chicago, Illinois: Moody, 1992), 11, 16.

6 Ron Whited, Driving a square peg into a round hole, *A Front Row View of The Church*, July 16, 2017, retrieved from https://ronwhited.wordpress.com/.

7 Hanna Rosin, "Beyond 2000: A Self-Made Deity," *Washington Post*, Jan.18, 2000. Retrieved from https://www.washingtonpost.com/wp-srv/WPcap/2000-01/18/066r-011800-idx.html.

8 C.S. Lewis, Mere Christianity, A Revised and Amplified Edition, (New York: NY: Harper Collins, 2015), 31 (e-kindle).

9 Michelle Van Loon, How to Fight Peer Pressure Culture in Our Churches, *Christianity Today*, June 17, 2021, retrieved from https://www.christianitytoday.com/pastors/2021/june-web-exclusives/how-to-fight-peer-pressure-culture-in-our-churches.html.

10 John Lennox and Michael Ruse (debaters), *The Big Debate, Episode #4*, YouTube. Retrieved from https://www.premierchristianradio.com/Shows/Saturday/Unbelievable/Videos/Michael-Ruse-vs-John-Lennox-Science-faith-and-the-evidence-for-God, (40:05-40:16).

11 Anthony C. Thiselton, *First Epistle to the Corinthians: A Commentary on the Greek Text*, (Grand Rapids, Michigan: Wm. B. Eerdmans, 2000), 1064.

12 Stone, *op. cit.*, 8.

13 WJLA Staff, 'Amen and a-woman': Congressman ends opening prayer in interesting fashion, ABC, Channel 7 - WJLA news video, January 4, 2021. Retrieved from https://wjla.com/news/local/amen-awomen-congressman-ends-opening-prayer-cleaver.

14 Brad Sylvester, Fact Check: Did Einstein Say, 'The Difference Between Stupidity And Genius Is That Genius Has Its Limits'? *Check Your Fact*, Nov 7, 2019, retrieved from https://checkyourfact.com/2019/11/07/fact-check-albert-einstein-difference-stupidity-genius-limits/.

15 Editors, The Spirit of the RMS Titanic: And the Band Played On, *Strings*, February 16, 2012, retrieved from https://stringsmagazine.com/the-spirit-of-the-rms-titanic-and-the-band-played-on/.

16 Joseph H. Gilmore, He Leadeth Me (2nd stanza), Public Domain, 1862.

## CHAPTER 4

1 Meister Eckhart (1260–1327), An influential priest of the Dominican order, theologian, lecturer, and Prior, retrieved from https://www.biographyonline.ne/spiritual/meister-eckhart.html and https://www.azquotes.com/quotes/topics/finding-god.html.

END NOTES

² Dr. Jim Denison, The Key to True Peace, The Dr. Jim Denison Resource Library, July 14, 2019, retrieved from https://www.jimdenisonlibrary.org/the-key-to-true-peace/.

³ Tom Schulman, *Dead Poet's Society,* Touchstone Pictures, 1989Wesley Wildman, Review by SC of Paul Tillich's The Courage to Be, Paul Tillich Resources, 1994, retrieved from http://people.bu.edu/wwildman/tillich/resources/review_tillich-paul_couragetobe.htm#Review_by_SC.Daniel Schorn.

⁴ Tom Brady Talks To Steve Kroft (Transcript, Tom Brady, Part 3), 60 Minutes, Nov 4, 2005, retrieved from https://www.cbsnews.com/news/transcript-tom-brady-part-3/.

⁵ Dorothy L. Sayers, an excerpt from *The Other Six Deadly Sins: Sloth*, An Address given to the Public Morality Council at Caxton Hall, Westminster, October 23rd, 1941, retrieved from http://www.lectionarycentral.com/trinity07/Sayers.html.

⁶ Tariq Malik, "'Cosmos: A Spacetime Odyssey' Reboots Carl Sagan's Landmark TV Series on Fox Tonight," *Space.com*, March 09, 2014, Retrieved from https://www.space.com/24997-cosmos-reboot-carl-sagan-spacetime-odyssey.html.

⁷ Jeremy Kloppenborg, "Philosophy 'The love of Wisdom' - Inspiring Thoughts," Retrieved from https://www.jeremykloppenborg.com/blog.

⁸ Guinness, *op. cit.,* 13–14.

⁹ Carl Ballou, USCCB after 9 killed in San Jose shooting: "Something fundamentally broken in our society," The Catholic World Report, May 27, 2021, retrieved from https://www.catholicworldreport.com/2021/05/26/usccb-after-9-killed-in-san-jose-shooting-something-fundamentally-broken-in-our-society/.

¹⁰ George Lucas (story), Menno Meyjes, and Jeffrey Boam, Indiana, Jones and the Last Crusade, Paramount Pictures, May 24, 1989.

¹¹ Lewis, *op. cit.,* 49.

## CHAPTER 5

¹ Keith Harris, Knowing God, *Life in the Rock*, July 23, 2019, retrieved from https://www.lifeintherock.org/single-post/2019/07/23/knowing-god.

² St. Athanasius, *On the Incarnation: De Incarnatione Verbi Dei*, Kindle Edition, (C.R. Draper, CreateSpace Publishing, 2017), 22.

³ David Van Biema, God vs. Science, Time, Nov 5, 2006. Retrieved from http://content.time.com/time/magazine/article/0,9171,1555132-1,00.html.

⁴ Leo Graham (2008). The God Delusion. *TEACH Journal of Christian Education*, 2(1), 48–50. Retrieved from https://research.avondale.edu.au/teach/vol2/iss1/12.

⁵ Ron Almberg, Explaining God, Weatherstone's Blog, retrieved from https://weatherstone61.wordpress.com/tag/art-linkletter/.

⁶ Nik Ripken, *The Insanity of God: A True Story of Faith Resurrected* (Nashville, TN: B and H Publishing Group, 2013), 178–179.

⁷ S.M. Lockridge, *Where a Sick Man Can Get Well,* retrieved from https://youtuberead.com/s-m-lockridge-where.

⁸ Claire Carroll, Biography of Albert Camus, French-Algerian Philosopher and Author, *ThoughtCo*, May 1, 2020, retrieved from https://www.thoughtco.com/biography-of-albert-camus-philosopher-author-4843862.

⁹ Albert Camus, Quotable Quotes, *Goodreads*, retrieved from https://www.goodreads.com/quotes/42024-i-would-rather-live-my-life-as-if-there-is.

¹⁰ Mitch Albom, *Have A Little Faith*, (New York, NY: Hyperion, 2009), 77–79.

¹¹ A.W. Tozer, *The Knowledge of the Holy*, (New York: HarperCollins, 1961), viii, 1–2.

¹² Ben Hughes, *When God Breaks In*, (Shippensburg, PA: Destiny Image, 2019), 9, 11.

¹³ Thomas, R.L., *Hebrew-Aramaic Dictionary of the New American Standard Exhaustive Concordance,* Updated Version, (La Habra, California: The Lockman Foundation, 1998), 3048.

¹⁴ Healing and Revival Press Staff, *Remain in Me and I in You – Biography of Andrew Murray,* Healing and Revival Press, retrieved from https://healingandrevival.com/BioAMurray.htm.

¹⁵ David H. Roper, For His Time, *Our Daily Bread Ministries*, March 4, 2021, retrieved from https://odb.org/US/2016/03/04/for-his-time.

¹⁶ Philip Yancy, *What Good Is God? In Search of a Faith That Matters*, (New York, NY: Jericho Books, 2010), 136–137.

¹⁷ Henry Blackaby, *Experiencing the Spirit: The Power of Pentecost Every Day,* Good Reads. Retrieved from https://www.goodreads.com/author/quotes/21025.Henry_T_Blackaby.

## CHAPTER 6

[1] St. Athanasius, *On the Incarnation: De Incarnatione Verbi Dei*, Kindle Edition, (C.R. Draper, CreateSpace Publishing, 2017), 40.

[2] Lucado, Max. *In the Manger*, Kindle Edition, (Nashville, Tennessee: Thomas Nelson, 2012), 102–103.

[3] Carl Sagan, *Pale Blue Dot: A Vision of the Human Future in Space*, (New York: Ballentine Books, 1994), 6.

[4] St. Athanasius, *op. cit.,* title page.

[5] Larry Getlen, The untold story of how the buried Chilean miners survived, *N.Y. Post*, October 11, 2014, Retrieved from https://nypost.com/2014/10/11/how-the-chilean-miners-men-survived-for-69-days-beneath-the-earths-surface/.

[6] Cesar Illiano and Terry Wade, Chilean miners freed in 'miracle' rescue, *Reuters*, October 12, 2010, Retrieved from https://www.reuters.com/article/idINIndia-52154920101013.

[7] Ibid.

## CHAPTER 7

[1] Juliana LaBianca, 18 Hilarious Parenting Stories That Will Make You Laugh Out Loud, Reader's Digest Newsletter, Updated: Jul. 10, 2018, retrieved from https://www.rd.com/list/hilarious-parenting-true-stories/.

[2] A.W. Tozer, *The Pursuit of God*, (Alberta, Canada: Horizon House, 1976), 11.

[3] Barry Kauffman, In Times Like These, *Hymns with a Message*, Sept 28, 2014, retrieved from http://barryshymns.blogspot.com/2014/09/in-times-like-these.html.

[4] R.C. Sproul, *The Holiness of God*, (Wheaton, IL: Tyndale House, 1985), 197.

[5] Corrie ten Boom, (FACEBOOK Post), The Corrie ten Boom Museum, Aug 9, 2018, retrieved from https://www.facebook.com/corrietenboommuseum/posts/if-you-look-at-the-world-youll-be-distressed-if-you-look-within-youll-be-depress/2221117351238687/.

[6] Harold J. Chadwick, editor, *The New Foxe's Book of Martyrs 1001*.(Gainesville, Florida: Bridge-Logos, 2001), 117–119.

[7] Dargan Thompson, 20 Spurgeon Quotes That Show Why He Still Matters, Relevant Magazine, June 19, 2014, retrieved from

https://www.relevantmagazine.com/faith/20-spurgeon-quotes-show-why-he-still-matters/.

[8] Philip Yancy, *Rumors of Another World*, (Grand Rapids, Michigan: Zondervan, 2003), 69.

[9] Anne Pressley, A Bittersweet Mantle: I've Been So Lucky in My Life, *The Washington Post*, July 12, 1995, retrieved from https://www.washingtonpost.com/archive/sports/1995/07/12/a-bittersweet-mantle-ive-been-so-lucky-in-my-life/8a515213-1d9e-4287-ae28-92d1d961e4d8/.

[10] *Ibid.*

[11] Susannah Spurgeon, *A Basket of Summer Fruit*, Classic Christian Books, provided by CarrytheLight.io, 4, retrieved from https://www.yumpu.com/en/document/read/62825684/a-basket-of-summer-fruit-susannah-spurgeon.

[12] Mark Batterson, Whisper: *How to Hear the Voice of God*, (Colorado Springs: Multnomah, 2017), 184.

[13] David Van Biema, "Behind America's Different Perceptions of God," Time, Oct. 23, 2006, Retrieved from http://content.time.com/time/nation/article/0,8599,1549413,00.html.

[14] Stephen Thompson, Is There A God? *The AV Club*, 10/09/02, retrieved from https://www.avclub.com/is-there-a-god-1798208251.

[15] *Ibid.*

[16] Ellen Vaughn, *Becoming Elisabeth Elliot*, (Nashville, Tennessee: B & H Publishing Group, 2020), 15.

[17] Wonder Woman, *WW84*, Warner Brothers Picture, Dec 25, 2020.

[18] Ophelia Benson and Jeremy Stangroom, *Why Truth Matters,* (New York, NY: Continuum Books, 2006), 21.

[19] Philip A. Pecorino, *Introduction to Philosophy — An Online Textbook*, (Queensborough Community College, CUNY), Steven Robinar quote, Retrieved from https://www.qcc.cuny.edu/socialsciences/ppecorino/intro_text/chapter%205%20epistemology/Why-Truth-Matters.htm.

# CHAPTER 8

[1] Sharon Jaynes, God Is Always Working in Your Behind-the-Scenes, Proverbs 31 Ministries, Dec 30, 2020, retrieved from

https://proverbs31.org/read/devotions/full-post/2020/12/30/god-is-always-working-in-your-behind-the-scenes.

² Hannah Whitall Smith, *The God of All Comfort*, (Chicago, IL: Moody Press, 1956 edition), 8.

## CHAPTER 9

¹ Wendell Berry, *Jayber Crow* (Washington DC: Counterpoint, 2001), 133

² C. Michael Hawn, History of Hymns: "He Leadeth Me: O Blessed Thought," *Discipleship Ministries: The United Methodist Church*, Mar 14, 2018, retrieved from https://www.umcdiscipleship.org/resources/history-of-hymns-he-leadeth-me-o-blessed-thought.

³ R. Kirby Godsey, *When We Talk about God...Let's Be Honest*, (Macon, Georgia: Smyth & Helwys, 1996), 13.

⁴ Randy Munter, Editor, Quotes by Famous Men, *The Old Time Gospel*, retrieved from http://theoldtimegospel.com/men/m_quotes.html.

⁵ Mark Galli and Ted Olsen, Editors, *131 Christians Everyone Should Know*, (Nashville, TN: Broadman and Holman, 2000), 73–75.

⁶ *Ibid*, 76–77.

⁷ Editors, John Bunyan, *Banner of Truth*, retrieved from https://banneroftruth.org/us/about/banner-authors/john-bunyan/.

⁸ 23 Most Famous Christian Converts (and 7 Famous De-Converts), *Online Christian Colleges*, retrieved from https://www.onlinechristiancolleges.com/famous-christian-converts-and-7-famous-de-converts/.

⁹ Brian "Head" Welch, *Save Me From Myself*, (New York, NY: HarperOne, 2007), x–xi.

¹⁰ Mike Lindell, *What Are the Odds? From Crack Addict to CEO*, (Chaska, Minnesota: Lindell Publishing, 2019), 1.

¹¹ *Ibid.*, 321.

## CHAPTER 10

¹ Daniel Wesley, 7 Perfect Love Quotes to Describe How You Feel About Him or Her, *Quote.com*, April 22, 2021, retrieved from https://www.quote.com/blog/77-perfect-love-quotes/.

² Debbi Levine, How Kids Define Love, *Navigating Change*, Dec 1, 2016, retrieved from http://www.debilevine.com/, 950.

³ R.C. Sproul, The Holy Love of God, *Tabletop Magazine* (Ligonier Ministries), July 1, 2014, retrieved from https://www.ligonier.org/learn/articles/holy-love-god/.

⁴ Candace Cameron Bure, "From the Heart," *Woman's Day*, February 2021, 21.

⁵ Debbie, "All Is Grace — A Thank You to Brennan Manning," *Two Minutes of Grace*, April 13, 2013, retrieved from https://twominutesofgrace.wordpress.com/tag/the-ragamuffin-gospel.

⁶ Guidepost, 10 Amazing Quotes About God's Love, retrieved from https://www.guideposts.org/faith-and-prayer/daily-devotions/10-amazing-quotes-about-gods-love.

⁷ Richard and Renee Stearns, *He Walks Among Us: Encounters with Christ in a Broken World*, (Nashville, TN: Thomas Nelson, 2013), 77.

# EPILOGUE

¹ C. Michael Hawn, History of Hymns: "Precious Lord, Take My Hand," *Discipleship Ministries, The United Methodist Church*, July 31, 2014, retrieved from https://www.umcdiscipleship.org/resources/history-of-hymns-precious-lord-take-my-hand.

² Thomas Dorsey, *Precious Lord, Take My Hand*, Public Domain, 1933.

www.ingramcontent.com/pod-product-compliance
Lightning Source LLC
Chambersburg PA
CBHW072149160426
43197CB00012B/2314